家族から見た「8・6」
語り継ぎたい10の証言

創価学会広島青年部 編

第三文明社

ヒロシマを忘れるな──。広島県北広島町の中国平和記念墓地公園に立つ世界平和祈願の碑。永遠の平和を築いていく人間の峻厳な精神が、（左から）「建設」「寛容」「勇気」「希望」「後継」「歓喜」のかたちで表現されている。フランスの彫刻家ルイ・デルブレ氏がすべての被爆者を追悼し、平和を誓う意義を6体の像に込めて制作した。「世界平和祈願之碑」の揮毫は中国を代表する作家、金庸氏の筆である

Don't forget Hiroshima —— World Peace Prayer Monument standing in Chugoku Peace Memorial Garden of Remembrance in Kita Hiroshima-cho, Hiroshima Prefecture. French sculptor Louis Debre produced six statues representing the commitment to peace that lies in the memory of all hibakusha. They express "building, tolerance, courage, hope, inheritance and joy (from left to right)." Leading Chinese writer Jin Yong wrote the inscription: World Peace Prayer Monument.

2015年7月19日、8000人の青年が広島に集い、第2回世界青年平和音楽祭が開催された（広島市の広島グリーンアリーナ）。被爆70年の節目から「核兵器廃絶へ　挑戦の10年」に向けて、若者たちの力強い一歩が踏み出された　　　　　　（ⒸSeikyo Shimbun）

The Second International Youth Music Festival for Peace was held at Hiroshima Green Arena drawing 8,000 youth from the Chugoku Region on July 19, 2015. This festival was a strong step by youth toward the "Ten-year Challenge – Nuclear Abolition," proposed to mark the 70th anniversary of the atomic bombing.

家族から見た「8・6」——語り継ぎたい10の証言

はじめに

原爆ドームは、今からちょうど百年前の一九一五年（大正四年）に、地元の特産品を展示する「広島県物産陳列館」として落成し、時代を経て、「広島県産業奨励館」へと改名されました。

そして一九四五年（昭和二十年）八月六日午前八時十五分、同館から南東約百六十メートル先、高度約六百メートルの上空で人類史上最初の原子爆弾が炸裂しました。

現在は世界遺産となった原爆ドームも、かつては存廃危機に揺れ動いた時期がありました。

広島市が、初めて原爆ドーム保存募金運動をスタートさせた六年も前の

一九六〇年（昭和三十五年）八月のこと。平和記念公園の「原爆の子の像」前で、ドーム保存を訴え募金と署名を呼びかける、わずか十人ほどの子どもたちがいました。

その年の四月、急性白血病のため亡くなった広島県安芸郡府中町の楮山ヒロ子さん（享年十六）の残した日記に胸を打たれた小・中・高校生の「広島折鶴の会」のメンバーでした。額に大粒の汗を浮かべながら配っていたそのビラには「20世紀以後は原爆慰霊碑の碑文と、あのいたいたしい原爆ドームだけが、いつまでも恐るべき原爆を世に伝えてくれるでしょう」との、ヒロ子さんの日記が引用されていました。

当時、原爆ドームに対する市民感情は好意的とは言えませんでした。被爆者の中でも議論が分かれ、新聞は撤去を主張し、広島市長、県知事らも解体論を唱えていました。しかし「広島折鶴の会」が最初に行動を開始し、各種団体や著名人の要請もあり、広島市議会は一九六六年（昭和四十一年）

七月、ついに原爆ドームの保存を全会一致で決議。わずか十人ほどの子どもたちから始まった運動が、燎原の火のごとく広がり、ドームの保存に結びついたということに、深い感動をおぼえます。

本書『家族から見た「8・6」――語り継ぎたい10の証言』は、広島の青年平和会議（青年平和委員会・女性平和文化会議・学生平和委員会）を中心とする青年が被爆者のご自宅等で体験をうかがい、まとめた被爆証言集です。

四人の被爆体験と、六組の被爆二世の方々からも親御さんの被爆体験をうかがうという、新しいエッセンスを加えました。

被爆体験は、語るほうも、私たち聞くほうも、心に痛みが走ります。本書で紹介されている「被爆者があまり体験を話さないのは、語り出したら涙が出るのと、表現の仕様がないほど悲惨で、むごい光景だったからです。人間性の輝きなど、まったく失われた暗黒世界、この世の地獄です。

それをどう表現したらいいのか、伝える術がないのです。被爆者は皆、そうした"心の傷"を負っています」との叫びは胸に迫るものがあります。

しかし、過去に背を向けず真摯に向き合い、"心の痛み"を持った人々こそ、戦争と核兵器のない世界を創る第一歩を踏み出せると確信します。

愚かな戦争の歴史は、人間が創ってきました。なれば、平和の歴史も、人間が創るしかありません。

その人間とは誰でしょうか。

それは、未来を生きる使命と責任のある"青年"ではないでしょうか。

原爆ドーム保存を求めて募金署名活動を行った、わずか十人ほどの子どもたちのような「平和への情熱」を燃やし続ける人が一人でもいる限り、歴史を変えることは可能で、その主役こそ昔も今も"青年"だと思うのです。

本書も青年が体験を直接聞き取り、また私ども創価学会広島青年平和会

議が、一九八九年（昭和六十四年）以来、百六十回を超す「平和のための広島学講座」を連続開催してきたのも、そこに眼目があります。

原爆投下から七十年が過ぎ、被爆者の平均年齢が八十歳を超えた現在、「どのように"継承"していくのか」を、あらゆる団体が最重要の課題として挙げています。

本書を通し、親から子へ、そして若き青年へ継承した核兵器廃絶への「ヒロシマの心」が、人類共通の普遍的な価値観へと昇華（しょうか）する一助になれば、これ以上の喜びはありません。

二〇一五年十月　被爆七十年の年に
　　　創価学会広島青年平和委員会委員長　淀屋君雄
　　　創価学会広島女性平和文化会議議長　平井幸恵

目　次　家族から見た「8・6」――語り継ぎたい10の証言

はじめに

　　　　　淀屋君雄／平井幸恵 ……… 3

聞いてください。
被爆者と家族の心の悲痛な叫びを。

　　　　　大江啓子／高阪正子 ……… 12

平和が一番。地道な対話による
平和勢力の拡大を切望します。

　　　　　池上弘三／池上純代／池上哲夫
　　　　　　　　　　　　　　……… 20

父母を奪い、
家族を分断した戦争。
悲劇を二度と繰り返さないで！
　　　　　　　太田立子 ……… 30

母は思い出したくない過去を
未来のために語り残してくれました。
　　　　勝乗　隆／勝乗美智子 ……… 40

若い方々には
「戦争は絶対しない」という
決意を固めてほしいと願っています。
　　　　　　中西佐知子 ……… 56

「今の幸せを大事にせにゃいけん」という
父の思いを、知ってほしい。

長谷徳友／長谷槌男 …… 66

言葉では表しきれないほど
悲惨ですが、それでも
語り伝えていかねばなりません。

藤井三千明／藤井和子 …… 74

被爆者の生きた証しを残すには、
もう時間がありません。

中村一俊 …… 84

生き恥をさらしてでも
伝え残したい
私の"二重の苦しみ"。

江川政市

核兵器だけはいけん、と
訴え続けるのが、
私の使命です。

冨田照夫

むすびにかえて

守安佑介／高橋丈夫

聞いてください。
被爆者と家族の心の悲痛な叫びを。

大江啓子さん
（おおえけいこ）

高阪正子さん
（こうさかまさこ）

（広島県廿日市市）

母が被爆した日

母・高阪正子の被爆体験を、私が知っとる限りお話しします。

一九四五年（昭和二十年）八月六日。十五歳だった母は、東洋工業（現在のマツダ）で働いていましたが、その日から建物疎開の手伝いで友人二人と出掛ける予定でした。

母は、七時五十分発の汽車に乗るため向洋駅（むかいなだ）に着きましたが、待ち合わせをしていた友人の一人が遅れてきたので、その汽車には間に合いませんでした。これが運命の分かれ目になったのです。間に合っていたら、爆心地付近にいて、助からなかったはずです。

母が被爆をしたのは、友人二人と広島駅から京橋側の土手を鶴見橋（爆心地から約一・八キロ）方向に歩いていた時です。

橋の手前まで来ると空襲警報が解除されたので、かぶっていた防空頭巾（ずきん）

13　大江啓子／高阪正子

を取って上空を見上げようとした瞬間、背後から強い光がはしってきて、気付いたら血まみれになっていました。その瞬間は不思議と痛みは無かったそうですが、「時間がたつにつれて痛みがひどくなった」と。

私は「お母さん、その時どうしたん？」とたずねてみました。すると母は「身体のことより、街がのうなってしもうたことが信じられんかった」と言いました。橋の手前の土手から見た街は、跡形も無かったそうです。橋の周辺にいた人々は皆、熱さから逃れようと川へ飛び込みました。それを見た友人が「私たちも川へ入ろう」と言い、母は「いや、入らん。東洋工業へ戻ろう」と促したそうですが、三人で比治山を目指して逃げました。比治山には大勢の人が避難していましたが、知り合いの社員と出会い、その人が母たちを宿舎に連れ帰ってくれましたが、宿舎のグラウンドにも被爆した人々がいて「ぎょうさん亡くなっとった」と。そこには、死体の

山ができあがっていたそうです。

　母は三次市出身で、広島には出稼ぎのために来ていました。被爆した母は、頭やうなじ、肘や膝下にひどい火傷を負い、ほどなく帰郷しました。一緒に被爆した友人とは別れ別れになり、後日、二人とも亡くなったのを知ったそうです。でも、二人がどんな状態で亡くなったかは「知らん」と言います。同時に被爆したわけですから、きっと死に際を知るのが怖かったんだと思います。

　母は二十七歳の時、やはり被爆者の父（故人）と結婚をし、私たちを育て、現在に至っています。八月六日が近づくと「原爆が夢に出てくる」そうで、今なお原爆は、母の心に棲みついとるんです。

　母の言葉で印象的だったのが、「原爆は受けとおて受けたんじゃないよ」。この悲痛な言葉を生み出した原爆の恐ろしさを、世界中の人々に知ってい

ただきたいのです。

被爆二世としての思い

　ここからは、私自身のことです。私は原爆投下から十二年後の一九五七年（昭和三十二年）四月四日に生まれました。広島で育った私は、幼い頃から原爆について聞かされることが多く、「自分は被爆二世なんじゃ」と自覚をしたのは、中学生になってからだったように思います。でも、すすんで他人に言うことはありませんでした。

　高校卒業後、社会人になって味わった悲しい経験があります。友人の知り合いが私のことを、「広島の人なら、親は被爆してるんじゃないの？」と言ったというのです。面識のない人がそう言ったと聞いただけで、私の心は深く傷つきました。

被爆二世として思うことが、たくさんあります。でもそれは、どれも一筋縄ではいかない感情です。例えば、どうして両親がいた広島市が原爆投下の標的にされなければよかったのかなど、といったことです。では、他の都市が標的になっていればよかったのかなど（もちろんそんな訳はありません）、考えても答えが出ないことばかりです。

原爆というものは、戦争というものは、七十年という年月を経てもなお、被害者だけでなく子孫までも苛み続けているのです。

被爆者や被爆二世に対する周囲の偏見や差別は以前より減り、共々に考えることができる環境が、徐々にですが、できつつあります。でも、被爆者や被爆二世が、今も定期検診を受けているのをご存じでしょうか？母が被爆直後に避難した比治山は現在、公園として整備されていますが、その一画に放射線影響研究所という施設があります。ここでは、原爆後遺

17　大江啓子／髙阪正子

症の発症がないかといった検査や研究をしています。しかも、検査が終わって結果が届くまで約一カ月もかかり、その間は被爆に関連した病気が見つかったらどうしようと、生きた心地がしないのです。

＊

　私が強く願うのは、被爆者の〝生の声〟を聞いてほしいということです。私の母もそうですが、被爆者の高齢化がどんどん進み〝生の声〟に触れる機会は年々、少なくなっています。
　この原稿を母に見せると、読みながら泣いていました。その夜は、「八月六日〟が夢に出てきた」そうです。これは、被爆者の〝心の声〟だと思います。
　被爆者、そして被爆二世の心の悲痛な叫びに、ぜひ耳を傾けていただきたい……。特に若い方々に、このことを強く期待します。

平和が一番。地道な対話による平和勢力の拡大を切望します。

池上弘三（いけがみこうぞう）さん

池上哲夫（いけがみてつお）さん

池上純代（いけがみすみよ）さん

（広島県福山市）

父の体験を聞いて

池上弘三

　父（池上哲夫）から被爆のことを初めて聞いたのは、小学生の時。反戦出版の制作ということで父に取材をした時です。当時の私は、父の四十年以上も前の被爆体験に憤りと理不尽を感じながら、原稿を書いたのを覚えています。

　昭和五年（一九三〇年）八月五日生まれの父は、十五歳の誕生日の翌日に被爆し、被爆七十年の今年（二〇一五年）の八月五日に八十五歳になりました。

　私自身、被爆二世ということでの差別やいじめもなく、原爆の後遺症もありませんでした。あまりにも普通に過ごしてきました。

胎内被爆でダウン症の障害を持った叔父の史夫（ふーちゃん）を福山に引き取り、二十四年間一緒に暮らしました。音楽が得意だったふーちゃん。知能は小学校低学年くらいでしたが、クラシックが大好きで、絶対音感があり、一度耳で聴いた曲は譜面なしでアコーディオンで弾くことができました。

ふーちゃんは平成二十一年（二〇〇九年）、六十三歳で亡くなりました。私たちの子ども二人にとって、ふーちゃんと暮らしたことは、まさに生きた平和学習そのものだったと思います。

原爆について多くを語らなかった父が、重い口を開いて被爆体験を残すことに協力してくれたのは、今の日本の平和がいつまでも続くのを願ってのことだと思います。

平和が一番。そのためにも地道な対話を通して、平和勢力を

― 拡大していくことが大切と痛感します。

今回、妻（純代）と相談し、改めて父の被爆体験を後世に残し伝えるべく、父の語り口のままに、その悲痛な体験を紹介します。

十五歳の誕生日の翌日に被爆した私　　池上哲夫

わしの生まれは呉市の本通九丁目の電車通り。親父が警察官で転勤が多く、己斐（こい）（現在の広島市西区己斐）へ移り、二、三年生まで己斐小学校（当時は国民学校）で、それから大芝（現在の広島市西区大芝）に移り、大芝小学校、崇徳（そうとく）中学校へ通ったんよ。

この時分は本土への空襲が増え、お偉いさんたちが「こりゃ負けるぞ」って思いよったんじゃろ、生徒は防空要員として駆り出された。勉強

なんか二の次で、家が学校に近い生徒は、防空要員として学校へ毎日通ってね。

原爆が投下される前は、空襲はほとんどなかったね。海軍の拠点だった呉があったけ、呉のほうへアメリカの飛行機がいっぱい行ったんよ。「こりゃ広島にゃ来やせんで」と思うて皆が高をくくっとった。ほしたら、広島に……。

被爆したんは、十五歳の誕生日の翌日だった……。

そん時、わしは学校前の土手におったんよ。学校が始まるんが八時三十分じゃけ、同級生たちと一緒に待っとった。十何人か、おったがね。暑いんで、そのうちの数人は泳ぎよったよ、太田川でね。

原爆が落とされたんが八時十五分というのは後で知ったことじゃが、わしは見よったんよ、原爆を落とす飛行機を。空襲警報が解除されてから来

たんよね、飛行機が。

突然じゃけ、敵の飛行機とは思わんかった。一機だけ見えたんじゃが、牛田の上のほうを通って、広島上空を通ってね、岩国のほうに向かっとった……。

「こりゃ、おかしいぞ」と思いよったんじゃが、突然、頭が熱くなりよった。それが原子爆弾が爆発した瞬間で、わしにとっては「熱い」と思うた時や。かぶっとった学生帽は飛んでしまっていて、髪の毛が燃えとる。もう、何が起きたか、分からんかった。まだ飛行機の爆音がしていたんで川に入る準備だけはしとったが、川で泳ぎよった友達なんかは皆、ひどい火傷を負うとった。皮膚がべろーっと、全部剝けた者もおった。即死した者はおらなんだが、目も当てられんほど、ひどい状態じゃった。わしは体を動かすことができたんで、そのまま家に逃げ帰ったんよ。

裸で泳いでいた友達は、二、三日して死んどる者が多いんよ。建物疎開

の手伝いで街に出とったクラスメートも、多く死んだんよ。わしが防空要員でなかったら、建物疎開に行ってきっと死んどった。当時は一クラス四十人ほどおって、四学級あった同級生の四分の三ほどが、原爆で亡くなっとる。

被爆直後は、どこもかしこも、もう煙で見やせなんだわ。爆心地の方角はわーっと煙が上がっていて、楠木町のほうから歩いて来た人が川で血を洗い流しとった光景が、この世のこととは思えんほど強い印象として残っとる。

原爆が落ちた時は、校舎はまだ助かっとった。じゃが、ずっと周囲が焼けとって、後に校舎も類焼で失った。わしの家もやられとってね。当時は親父が勤めとった自動車学校の官舎に住んどったが、電気がつかんのよ。しばらくの間、防空壕で寝起きしよった。何日続いたか、はっきりは覚えてないんじゃがね。

胎内被爆した弟

　お母さんが火傷をひどく心配したが、原爆に遭うた大勢の人に比べたら症状は軽かったほうだと思う。火傷は後頭部から首筋、背中、それに眼鏡をかけていたんでその後ろ側の皮膚などで、被爆したのが夏場だったんで汗が流れると痛み、やがて化膿による痛みもあって、治るのにだいぶん長くかかったよ。

　中国新聞社（上流川町、現在の中区胡町）の隣に銀行があって、その屋上が治療場で、そこで何日か診てもらった。後年、前立腺のがんが出たが、原爆症の関係は薄いということじゃった。

　一緒に暮らしとったのは父母と子ども四人。じゃけ、お母さんは身ご

もっとった。戦後に生まれた弟の史夫（ふーちゃん）は胎内被爆でダウン症じゃった。年の離れた弟と、子育てに苦労するお母さんの姿を見るたび、わしは原爆を思い出さずにはおれんかったよ。お母さんは、七十四歳の時にがんで亡くなった。一番の被害者は、この二人じゃけ。お母さんは、七十四歳の時にがんで亡くなったよ。

敗戦後、親父は広島で勤務し、老衰で亡くなった。九十二歳じゃった。わしらの家族の場合、被爆者だからという差別、偏見はなかったように思う。

原爆被害に遭ったことに対しての怒りや悔しさはあったが、当時の感情は忘れてしもうたよ。

父を奪い、
家族を分断した戦争。
悲劇を二度と繰り返さないで！

太田立子(おおたたつこ)さん

（広島県廿日市市）

神戸で空襲に遭い、母と二人の姉を失う

わが家は、父母と子どもが八人。長男以外の七人は女で、私が末っ子です。私が物心ついた頃は戦争のさなかで、うち一人は結婚で、二人は疎開や親戚の養女になって家を出ていました。灘（神戸市）の家には、兵役を終えて会社勤めをしていた父、母と三人の姉と私が暮らしていました。

国民学校初等科に通うようになると空襲が激しくなり、勉強どころじゃありませんでした。一年生だった一九四五年（昭和二十年）六月六日、父が勤めに出掛けた後の午前九時頃……米軍の空襲が始まりました。焼夷弾をドガンドガンと落とし、それがバーンと破裂して、辺りが火の海になりました。母を呼びましたが返事はなく、そばにいた六年生の姉に手を引かれて、火と煙の海の中を避難場所目指して走って逃げました。

太田立子

途中で、火傷をして「水をください」と言う人に出会ったり、怪我をしてその場にうずくまったままの人も見かけましたが、手を差し伸べることもできず、逃げるので精いっぱいでした。避難場所に着き、母や他の姉たちがいないことを知って、不安が増しました。その夜は「お母さんは死んだ」と泣きわめいて、姉を困らせたそうです。

二日後、姉と一緒に家に向かいました。家は焼けてしまっていました。姉が「母が着ていた服を覚えている」と言うので、それを頼りに母の姿を探しました。周囲でも棒を手に焼け跡を掘り返して家族を探す姿が多く見られ、辺り一面に言いようのない異臭が漂っていました。結局、母や二人の姉の遺体は見つかりませんでした。

避難場所には一週間いましたが、着のみ着のままで、乾パン一袋とヤカンの水だけで飢えをしのぎました。

原爆で父が亡くなる

戦争によるわが家の悲劇は、まだ続きました。父と姉二人と私は、母親の実家がある広島県高田郡八千代町（現在の安芸高田市八千代町）に避難、疎開(かい)しました。その後、姉の一人は三原の紡績工場の寮に入りました。

広島に原爆が落とされた時、私がいた八千代町でも地響きがしました。驚いて外に出て空を見上げると、わーっと真っ黒い雲が上ったのが見えました。その日（八月六日）、父は用事で広島に出掛けていました。国民学校初等科四年生の姉と一年生の私が留守番をしていましたが、父のことが心配になって二人で外に出ました。道路の端に座っていたら、灰が混じった黒い雨が降ってきました。でも、それが放射能を含んだ雨だったことなど、幼い子どもが知るよしもありません。

黒い雨に打たれながら、私たちは広島方面からやってくるトラックを待

太田立子

ちました。トラックには、火傷をした人がたくさん乗っていました。トラックを止め「山門春二（やまかどはるじ）、おりませんか。おったら、ここで降りてください」と、泣きながら父の名前を呼びました。でも、父は現れませんでした。
そのうち、近所のおじさんが「春さん、死んだで。ピカ（原爆）で死んだ」と知らせてくれました。それを聞いて、私ら姉妹はただ泣くばかりでした。後で広島市内へ行ったのですが、手をつないでもらって廃墟（はいきょ）の中を歩いたり、おんぶしてもらった記憶が残っています。亡くなった人の姿は見掛けなかったので、被爆直後ではなかったと思いますが、鼻をつく臭いだけ残っていました。この時も、父の遺体は見つかりませんでした。

四十八歳で「原爆手帳」をもらう

両親を亡くし、兄は戦地に行ったまま。結局、私はつてを頼りに居所を

34

転々とする人生を送るはめになったのです。まず、長女が嫁いでいた四国の今治市へ向かいました。義兄が迎えに来てくれたのですが、列車の乗り継ぎの関係で途中、広島市内に入りました。被爆後一週間ほどたっていましたが、まだ異臭は抜けていませんでした。広島駅で野宿し、明くる日の朝、尾道まで行き、そこで終戦を知ったのです。

戦地から帰ってきた兄が、私と四つ年上の姉を引き取り、神戸の塩屋町で一緒に暮らしたのはわずか一年ほど。二人の妹の面倒をみるほどの収入がなかったのです。それで、私は兄の戦友の家に預けられることになって熊本県の人吉市へ。その兄は、山口県の炭鉱で働いていた時に、キジア台風（一九五〇年九月）による土砂崩れで亡くなりました。兄は終戦まで戦地にいて、その間に父母と二人の妹を失い、敗戦の失意の中で必死に生きようとしてきたあげく、事故死したのです。その人生を思うと、戦争に対する怒りが込み上げてきます。

太田立子

熊本には十八歳までいて、叔母たちを頼って広島に来ました。流川で一カ月、佐伯郡永原（現在の廿日市市永原）で約二年暮らしました。永原ではもっぱら農業の手伝いをしていましたが、その時、縁あって夫と知り合い、結婚することになったのです。当時、夫は林業の仕事をやっていましたが、後に会社勤めをし、六十三歳で病死しました。子どもは男の子が二人で、私は次男と同居しています。

長男の結婚式の時、四国の義兄が私を引き取りに来た時の話をしたついでに「立子は原爆手帳（被爆者健康手帳）をもらっているのか？」とたずねてきました。被爆当時は初等科一年生で、四十年も前のことです。私は黒い雨を浴びたし、父の遺体を探すために広島市内に行った覚えがあり、被爆一週間後には四国の義兄と一緒に市内を歩き、広島駅で野宿しました。いわゆる〝入市被爆〟の対象者ということは分かっていました。私は、そ

れまでは健康だったし、学校も出てないから書くこともようせんかったので、手続きをしていませんでした。でも、夫が手伝うと言ってくれたので、申請してみることにしました。

申請には、広島市に入った日と、その理由を作文にして三通出しました。一通は広島県庁に、もう一通は義兄用に愛媛県庁に提出しました。それに国民学校初等科の通学証明が必要で、高田郡の教育委員会の倉庫に残っていた名簿、今治の小学校の受け入れ証明などを探してもらい、保証人になってくれる人もいたので原爆手帳を発行してもらえたのです。四国の義兄も入市被爆が認められ、手帳を発行してもらいましたが、それから二年ほどで亡くなりました。一緒に黒い雨を浴びた四歳上の姉は、疎開していたという理由で手帳がもらえませんでした。

四十八歳で手帳を手にした時、私はなぜか、亡くなった両親からのご褒美(び)のような気がしたものです。父も母も遺体すら残していないのですから、

37　太田立子

私にとって唯一の形見のように思えました。

＊

 子どもの頃は髪の毛が抜けやすかったり、吐き気がしたりという程度で、それが被爆によるものかどうかはっきりしません。十年ほど前、甲状腺がんの手術をしましたが、これも被爆との関係かどうかはっきりしていません。ただ、七十歳を超えてから、骨折したり眼病になったり、体のあちこちが弱っています。年のせいという見方もできますが、被爆も影響しているのではないかという不安もちょっぴりあります。
 二人の子どもは被爆二世ということになるわけですが、その手続きをしたほうがよいと周囲に勧められても、二人ともしようとしません。子どもたちなりの考えがあってのことだと思いますが、私はそれを尊重してあげたいですね。少なくとも、私が味わった悲劇を繰り返すことなく、こうして一緒に暮らしていられるのですから……。今は時代が良くなって、幸せ

ですよね。

母は思い出したくない過去を未来のために語り残してくれました。

勝乗　隆 さん

勝乗美智子 さん

（広島市安佐北区）

母の被爆体験と反戦への思い　　　勝乗　隆

　私が幼い頃、母・美智子の足がひび割れているのを疑問に思っていました。後に母が「はだしで必死に逃げたんよ。死体が川に浮いて、たくさん死んどった」と壮絶な体験を語る姿に、原爆の威力や影響力とは、むごくて残酷なものだと感じたのを覚えています。

　母は、二〇一四年（平成二十六年）一月に心筋梗塞になって、その後に腰を骨折しました。圧迫骨折で背骨を四カ所、腰は一カ所骨折しました。七十歳過ぎてから体はぼろぼろで、身長が十六センチ縮みました。

「これが原爆による因果関係か、それとも老化か、分かりませ

ん。だから、原爆に遭ったからだと思わないようにしています」と、母は言っています。今まで、親子で病気のことが原因で口げんかしたこともありました。でも、原爆のことには触れません。きっと、思い出したくもない過去だったのでしょう。

その母が、自らの被爆体験を人に話すようになったのは、平成十九年から始めたヒロシマピースボランティア（広島平和記念資料館の展示解説や平和記念公園の慰霊碑等の解説を行う）がきっかけだったようです。

母は心筋梗塞になってから、ピースボランティアを休んでいます。生きがいだったピースボランティアができなくなって、とても残念がっています。でも、母の被爆体験と反戦への思いを、このような形で残すことができ、息子として満足しています

す。
　　母がやっとの思いで書き上げた被爆体験をもとに、私が聞き
　取りしたものを含め、紹介させていただきます。

被爆した日のこと　　　　　　　　勝乗美智子

　私は広島市中区昭和町（爆心地から一・六キロ）の自宅で国民学校三年生（八歳）の時に被爆しました。当時、国の方針で三年生以上は疎開することになっていました。縁故疎開と集団疎開があり、田舎に親戚がいる人は縁故疎開、いない人は集団疎開ということでした。私は遠い親戚をたよって祖母と二人で縁故疎開しました。疎開先は安佐郡福木村（現在の広島市東区）で、福木国民学校に通学していました。そこには集団疎開の生徒が大勢いて、物がない時代だったので、児童全員がはだしで登下校していたんです。

八月五日の夜、父が私を迎えに来ました。母の実家に疎開し直すことになったからです。その夜、私は父に連れられ約十キロの夜道を、歩いて昭和町の自宅に帰りました。自宅に着いたのは夜でしたが、私は疲れ果ててすぐ寝てしまいました。

六日、両親と私、五歳の弟が朝食を済ませた後、それぞれ別の部屋にいました。私は、隣家の子に本を借りていたので、返しに行こうと準備していました。襖（ふすま）を開けた途端、バタバタと襖や障子が倒れかかっていたのか記憶にないんです。気が付くと、はるか向こうに小さな明かりが見えました。その下敷きになりましたが、どれくらい下敷きになっていたのか記憶にないんです。気が付くと、はるか向こうに小さな明かりが見えました。そこまで行けば外に出られるんじゃないかと思って、瓦礫（がれき）の中を這（は）って外に出ました。

被爆した瞬間、音は聞いていません。後で皆が、ピカッと光って、ドー

ンと音がしたので「ピカドン」と呼んでいましたが、私は家の中にいたので光にも音にも気が付きませんでした。最初は「わが家にだけ爆弾が落ちた」と思っていました。二階建ての家は、ぺしゃんこになっていました。倒れた家の中から「助けてー、ここにおる。助けてー」と叫ぶ母と弟の声がしました。父の姿は見えましたが、左手を敷居と鴨居に挟まれて、しゃがんだまま身動きができないんです。「誰か助けてちょうだいって呼んでおいで！」と、父が言いました。

しばらく家の周りをぐるぐる回っていたり、外にいた人は吹き飛ばされて、助けてくれそうな人はいません。戻って「父さん誰もおってないよー」と言うと、父がそばにあった鉄の棒を「取ってちょうだい」って。それを渡すと、敷居と鴨居の間に差し込みました。死にもの狂いだったんでしょうね。しゃがんだままで、隙

間をこじ開け、左手を抜いて自由の身になりました。

それから二人で「助けて！　助けて！」と叫ぶ母と弟の声をたよりに必死に瓦礫をかきわけて探したのですが、声だけして、全然姿が見えません。そのうち、火の手が上がりました。火はあっという間に燃え広がり、私の服に火の粉が飛んできて、服が燃え出しました。父がすぐ消してくれ、そばに転がっていた夏布団を防火用水につけてびしょびしょにして、それを被って父と私は火の中をはだしで逃げていきました。母と弟は生きたまま、焼け死んだのです。

当時は、どの家の玄関先にも、防火用水があったのです。爆弾が落ちたら、すぐに消せるようにと。でも、原爆が落とされた時は、どの家も朝食の準備中だったり、食後の残り火があったんでしょう。あちこちで火の手が上がっていました。それに自然発火ですね。あの原爆のすごい熱線、投

下直後の爆心地の地表の温度は三〜四千度もあったと言われます。それによる自然発火もあったのでしょう。ぺしゃんこになった建物や燃え盛る瓦礫の中を、父と二人で比治山（ひじやま）を目指して逃げました。

途中、外にいた人は皆、吹き飛ばされていました。家の中にいた人は下敷きになって、そのまま焼け死んでいました。「助けてー、助けてー」という叫び声も耳にしましたが、どうにもなりません。比治山橋までたどり着くと、川の中にたくさんの人が入っているのが見えました。飛び込んでいる人も大勢いました。よく見ると、死体が重なり合って浮かんでいました。橋の両側にも、積み重なって人が倒れていました。黒焦（こ）げの人、皮膚がずるむけの人とか。

怖くなって、比治山橋を渡って四キロ離れた東雲町（しののめ）（現在の広島市南区東雲）の葡萄（ぶどう）畑まで逃げました。そこには、たくさんの人が逃げてきていま

した。その夜は、そこで野宿しましたが、広島市内の方角を見たら、大きな火柱が赤々とあちこちに上っていました。夜、東雲の婦人会の方が炊き出しをしておむすびを配ってくれました。

被爆後の暮らし

次の日、父と二人で福木村へ向かうことにしました。ところが父は「足が立たない」って言うんです。家が潰れた時、しゃがんだままだったのが原因だったのかも知れませんが、よたよたと壁って歩く父の手をひいて歩いていると後からトラックが来たのでそれに乗せてもらい、やっとのことで福木村の祖母の家にたどり着きました。

その後、父も私も下痢をしたり、嘔吐したり、髪の毛が抜けたりしまし

近所のお医者さんは、「赤痢(せきり)の疑いがあるけど、よう分からん」と診断したんです。結局、後から思うに、原爆の急性障害じゃなかろうかと。その時は分からず、赤痢かもしれないと思っていました。当時は薬もないので、祖母と叔母が野に行ってドクダミ草を摘んで、それを薬代わりに飲んでいました。叔母は父の妹で、呉(くれ)の空襲で焼け出されて福木村に疎開していました。

　症状が落ち着いてから、父と祖母と叔母の三人で、母と弟の遺骨を探しに昭和町まで毎日出掛けました。燃え残りの瓦礫の中を、まず家がどこにあったのかを調べるのですが、辺り一面が瓦礫で目印になるようなものはありません。分からずじまいで、父だけが出掛けるようになりました。何日かして、父が遺骨だといって持ち帰ってきました。

　「原爆が落とされた広島には、七十年間は草木が生えない」と言われてい

ました。それで父は昭和町に戻らずに、福木村に小さな家を建てて三人で暮らしました。でも私が小学六年生の二学期の時、「ぼつぼつ、みんな広島に帰って来よってらしい。やっぱり帰ろう」と言い出しました。それで、父と祖母と私の三人で、昭和町の焼け跡にバラックを建てて帰ってきました。学校はまだ復興していないので、隣の学区の千田小学校に通いました。講堂は、ぐにゃぐにゃの鉄骨のままでした。同級生や近所の友達と、焼け跡のコンクリートのようなタイル張りのところで、ままごと遊びをしました。

　ちょっと土を掘ると、人骨が出てきました。でも骨を見ても、気持ち悪いとも嫌だとも思わなくなっていました。ラジオ体操で時々出掛けた比治山の麓(ふもと)には防空壕(ごう)がたくさん掘ってあり、そこで生活している人がいっぱいいました。被爆後、二、三年たっても、まだそんな光景が見られたので

子どもの頃は、被爆者ということでの差別は受けませんでした。なぜなら周囲の人たちは皆、被爆者だったので。

原爆手帳（被爆者健康手帳）は、一九七二年（昭和四十七年）にもらいました。私が三十五歳の時です。被爆者ということが分かると不都合なことが多かったので、周りでも、すぐにもらわない人がたくさんいました。結婚したのは二十二歳で、その前の二年ほどは、基町の第一生命ビルに勤めていました。父は特にこれという症状が現れることなく九十三歳まで生き、自宅で私がみとりました。

被爆者としての思い

ヒロシマピースボランティアをしていた時、修学旅行の小学生を受け持ちました。終了後、感想を話してくれたのですが、六年生の男の子が、「説明で印象に残ったのは、『戦争すると人間が人間の心をなくす』という言葉です。勝乗さんにとって平和とは何ですか？」と質問してきました。私が「あなたは、どう思いますか？」と聞くと、その男の子は「人を傷つけようとする心をなくすことが平和だと思います」と答えました。「ああ、分かってるんだな」と、私は思いました。

私たち戦争を体験した者にとっては、絶対に戦争をしないことが、すなわち〝平和〟だと思います。これには、理屈は不要です。被爆者があまり体験を話さないのは、語り出したら涙が出るのと、表現の仕様がないほど

悲惨で、むごい光景だったからです。人間性の輝きなど、まったく失われた暗黒世界、この世の地獄です。それをどう表現したらいいのか、伝える術(すべ)がないのです。だから結局、言わないようになるんです。これは被爆者の方々に共通することではないかと思います。

父が生きていた間、私も父も原爆の話は一切しませんでした。それをボランティアの先輩に話すと、「親子で、何で原爆の話をせんのんですか？」って言うのです。話せない、話さないのは、親子だからです。お互いに相手のことを思いやって、話題にできないのです。当時のことを語れば「あの時、何で助けられなかったのか」「自分が焼けてもいいから助ければ良かった」といった自責の念が、子どもだった私にすらあります。父は、もっとあったと思うんです。被爆者は皆、そうした〝心の傷〟を負っています。

私も、そんな思いから息子にも話したことはありませんでした。話したら先に涙が出て、当時を思い出すから話せない。

今は平和な時代だけれども、この平和をずっと維持していくには戦争のむごさとか悲惨さを語り継ぐことが大事だと思います。それが根っこにあれば、若い方々がいざという時に「戦争反対」の旗を揚げて立ち上がってくださると信じています。

若い方々には
「戦争は絶対しない」という
決意を固めてほしいと願っています。

中西佐知子(なかにしさちこ)さん

(広島県大竹市)

父から聞いた被爆体験

亡父・渡部まさとは、一九一四年（大正三年）に佐伯郡己斐町（現在の広島市西区己斐）で生まれ、尋常高等小学校を出た後、一九四一年（昭和十六年）年頃まで御用船（軍事目的で徴用された船舶）に乗っていたそうです。その後、己斐の田中冷蔵庫という会社に入社しました。

被爆したのは三十二歳の時で、被爆した場所は白島国民学校（現在の広島市中区西白島町）の近くだったそうです。会社から出先に向かっている時、突然、辺り一面が閃光に包まれたので、瞬間的に目と耳を押さえて近くの溝に飛び込みました。当時、空襲で爆弾が落ちてきた時は、そうするようにと言われていたようです。

その直後、ドーンとすごい音とともに爆風が襲ってきて、気が付くと裸

中西佐知子

同然の姿になっていました。近くにあったタオルを腰に当てて、会社に戻ろうと歩いていると、指先から皮膚が垂れ下がった人々の姿が目に入りました。

「怖かったのー」と父は言いましたが、その言葉には何もできなかったつらさ、虚しさといったものを私は感じました。会社に戻った父は、バターの缶を三つ手にして佐伯郡廿日市（現在の廿日市市）の自宅に向かいました。火傷の治療には油が良いということで、会社でもらったそうです。
父の火傷は背中でしたが、ケロイドにはなっていなかったように思います。

自宅に向かう途中は、悲惨な光景をたくさん目の当たりにしたようです。背中におんぶした赤ちゃんが亡くなっているのに気づいているかどうか分からない母親、水を欲しがる人、川に飛び込む人……。地獄のような状況

の中、廿日市まで歩いて帰ったそうですが、自宅にたどり着いたのは被爆翌日の八月七日でした。

私が二歳だった一九五〇年（昭和二十五年）、わが家は五日市（現在の広島市佐伯区五日市）の皆賀に引っ越しました。山のてっぺんにあったトタン屋根の古い倉庫を人が住めるようにした家でした。

その二年後から、父は唇にただれが見られるようになり、私はABCC（原爆障害調査委員会）の黒い車が毎週金曜日になると自宅に迎えに来たことをはっきり覚えています。父はそれに乗って出掛けて行き、帰りも送ってもらっていました。その間、何が行われていたのか、具体的に父から聞いた記憶はありませんが、原爆症のことではないかということは、うすうす感じていました。

わが家では朝になると、父の唇のただれに母がお湯で濡らしたガーゼを

当てるのが日課になっていました。そうして時間がたつと、父はようやく口を開けることができたのです。

叔母二人も被爆

父の妹たちも被爆しました。亡くなったのは、当時十七歳だったシズコという妹でした。女学校に通っていて、当日（六日）の夕方、実家の近所の人がリヤカーで連れ帰ってくれたそうです。皮膚がずるずるにむけてしまっていて、話はできたそうなのですが、翌七日の真夜中に息を引き取りました。

もう一人の妹・保子は当時二十歳で、電話の交換手をしていた会社で被爆しました。

原爆が落とされた八時十五分は休憩時間中で、控室にいたために助かっ

たそうです。すっごい音がしたので驚いて部屋を出て防空壕に避難し、だいぶたって防空壕から出てみたら、ガラスは全部割れて、ドアも立ってはいるけど全部外れていました。

帰宅途中に黒い雨が降ってきて、着ていた白いブラウスが真っ黒になり、洗濯しても色は落ちなかったそうです。

「あれはね、黒いあられ、じゃったよ」と、叔母は言いました。

さらに、こんなことも語っていました。

「ゴムの手袋を半分脱ぎかけたような、そういう状態の人がいっぱいおっちゃったよ」「道路はガラスの破片がいっぱいで、毎日、夕方になると死体を山にして焼く臭いがしていたよ」

「戦争は絶対にしたらいけんよ」

私が父から直接、被爆体験を聞いたのは二十歳前後だったように思いま

"原爆乙女"と呼ばれた姉

　私の六歳年上の姉は"原爆乙女"と呼ばれ、嫌でも原爆と向き合うことを強いられた時期がありましたが、私の場合はことさら話す必要性を感じずに過ごしてきました。
　ですから結婚に際しても、夫に父が被爆者だとか、私が被爆二世ということは話していませんでした。今にして思えば、「話さにゃいけんかったんかな」と……。
　私自身、幼い頃からちょっと体が弱いというか、バスによく酔っていた

すが、どこで聞いたかもはっきり覚えていません。ただ、父と二人だけの時、「どうじゃったん？」といった感じで聞き出したような気がします。
　父が亡くなったのは、昭和五十四年（一九七九年）でした。

という記憶があります。遠足で平和記念資料館に行く機会が二度ありましたが、バス酔いが嫌で二度とも行きませんでした。

息子には「母さんは広島にいるのに、平和記念資料館に行っとらんじゃ、いけんじゃろう」って言われています。

子どもの頃に遠足で平和記念資料館に行き、帰宅した時に「涙が出て、お昼のお弁当が食べられんかった。母さん、絶対行こうね」と言っていた息子は、もう三十二歳です。

二年前、甲状腺がんの手術をしました。それまではずっと元気だったので、私には被爆二世という自覚はほとんどと言ってよいほどありませんでした。

被爆七十年ということで、広島では若い方々が語り部となって被爆体験を後世に残す作業をしておられるのには頭が下がります。私は話が苦手な

ので、話す勇気がなかなか出ないのですが、誰かが語り継ぐことは大事だと痛感します。

　平和とは、「どんなことがあっても戦争は絶対しない」という決意を継続するなかにこそあるのだと思います。それに気付いてくださった若い方々の存在は、頼もしい限りです。

「今の幸せを大事にせにゃいけん」という父の思いを、知ってほしい。

長谷徳友さん

長谷槌男さん

(広島県竹原市)

体験に勝るものはない

長谷德友

父・長谷槌男の被爆体験を聞いて、私は世間一般のイメージとかなり落差があるのではないかと思いました。父は、過去の不幸を嘆くよりも、今の幸せを大事にしたいという気持ちのほうが強かったのではないか。だからこそ、自身の被爆体験というよりは、むしろ反戦の思いを伝えたかったのではないか、という気がしてなりません。

被爆者が抱えている思いもそれぞれ違い、被爆者と被爆二世の考え方も一様ではありません。私は子どもの頃、アトピー性皮膚炎だったので、もしかすると原爆症かと不安に思った時期がありましたが、大人になって治まりました。被爆者や被爆二

世の病気のすべてを原爆と結び付けて語るには、あまりにも長い年月が過ぎてしまいました。検診を受けても、お医者さんには、それが原爆のためなのか、持病なのか判断がつかないことが多いようです。

はっきり言えるのは、戦争が起こらなければ原爆も落とされなかったという事実です。

だから、広島の悲劇を繰り返さないためには、日本は絶対に戦争という状況へ踏み込んではならない、戦争を美化してはならないと思います。

父が「今の平和な日本が大事、今の幸せが大事」と言い続けてきた、その思いがようやく分かるようになってきました。

「お父さん、体験に勝(まさ)るものはないよね」。そう父に言ってあげたい。

あの日の悲惨な光景

長谷槌男

父が被爆したのは、十八歳の時でした。爆心地から四キロの三菱造機という会社（現在の広島市西区にあった）に勤労動員として従事していましたが、原子爆弾が落とされた八月六日の前日が日曜日だったので実家に帰っていました。翌日、広島駅から電車に乗って観音町で下車し、会社に向かって歩いていた時、被爆したのです。

その時の様子を語った父の言葉を、広島弁もそのままに記します。

"もうちょっと遅かったら、電車の中でやられとった。歩いて行きよったら、突然、バーンと音がしたので、とっさに田んぼの畦に伏せたわ。"お

かしいのぉ、照明弾を落としたんかの"と思って、おそるおそる見上げたら、草むらが燃えよるのよ。田んぼには、刈り取ったイネが掛けられとって、それが燃えよった。会社の方角を見たら、屋根がきれいに無うなって鉄骨だけ残っとった。そういう状態じゃけ、もう会社にも行けるじゃない。国道二号線を歩いて逃げたが、まるで地獄の一丁目みたいじゃった。皮膚がずるずるにただれた人が、列をなして歩いとった。ところは、皮膚がぼろぼろだった。

五日市に向かって歩いている間に、黒い雨が降った。どうにかこうにかで、国民学校にたどり着いた。介抱しよるところに行ったら「あんたはまだ若い、あっちへ行きんさい」って言われてね。じゃけ、また広島に引き返した。広島に戻ると、猿猴橋の鉄橋の枕木が燃えよる。

これは、言うまいと思うとったんじゃが、猿猴橋の土手に火傷した将校

がおっての、「戸板を運べ」って命令すんよ。当時、将校の言うことは絶対じゃったけ、言われるように運んだが、死体を運ぶのを手伝わされそうになったけ、途中で逃げたんよ。軍馬も皮膚がずるずるで、かわいそうじゃった。猿猴川は潮が引いとって、歩いて対岸に渡った。
　海田（現在の安芸郡海田町）から汽車が出とる言うけぇ、歩いてそこまで行った。若い時じゃけ、昼飯も食わずにね。汽車は、人でいっぱいじゃった。わしは、機関車の石炭を置くところにしがみついて家に向かった。
　家に着いたのは、夜の十一時頃じゃったと思う。帰ると、お袋や兄が「臭い、臭い」と言うんじゃ。まこと、火傷しとるけんね。皮膚が出とるところは、火傷しとる。近くの医者に診てもらっても分からん。四十度の熱が一週間くらい続いたが、それからは元気になった。

切実な思い

　原爆の後遺症かどうかは分からんけど、腹を切ってね。直腸が下に出て、手術した。今、目が黄斑変性で二カ月に一ぺん、病院で診てもらいに広島へ行きよる。わしも年だが、もうちと生きていなさい、と言われとるんじゃと、感謝しとる。

　当時は、ほんまにひどかった。戦争はいけんのう。どんなことがあっても、戦争はいけんで。女性が気の毒なよね。夫を亡くした人を「未亡人」って言いよったが、わしゃ、それには腹が立ったよね。

　誰も好きこのんで戦地へ夫を送ったわけじゃない。じゃけ、「軍国主義」というのは、いけん」と、つくづく思ったよ。これは、わしの考えじゃが、もし日本が戦争に勝っとったら、今の日本はなかったと思うで。

わしはこれまで、原爆や戦争の話をしてこんかった。結婚当時、家内にも被爆したことは言わんかった。被爆したのを知った時も、家内は「原爆受けたんね」って言う程度で、偏見を持たんかった。はっきり言って、これには助けられたんよ。知られたくなかったわけじゃなく、話そうという感覚がなかった。被爆したことが、いいとか悪いとか、悪く見られるとか差別されるとかが、なかったんよ。
身内がそう思ってくれるだけで幸せで、他人がどう思うかは別問題よ。
今、わしは幸せよ。

言葉では表しきれないほど悲惨ですが、それでも語り伝えていかねばなりません。

藤井三千明 さん

藤井和子 さん

(広島県福山市)

入市被爆なんて知らなかった

藤井三千明

広島市内の陸軍被服支廠に勤めていた私は、原爆が落とされた八月六日は休暇をもらって福山の実家に帰っていました。

工場では陸軍の軍人の服、靴、帽子、シャツなどを作っていて、従業員は二千五百人くらいいました。戦争中だから休暇をもらうのがひと苦労で、例えば、こんなこともしたんです。それは、以前届いた手紙の使用済み切手を濡らして、はがすわけです。

そして、「チチキトク」とか「ハハキトク」と自分で手紙を書いて、はがした切手を貼り直して、さも届いたように細工してね。それを班長の所へ持っていくと、帰らしてくれるんよ。たまたま被爆の前日の五日に、どうしても実家に帰りたくなって、その手を使って休暇をとった。ただ帰りたくて、仕方がなかったんよ。

胸騒ぎがしたんじゃろうな。もし帰らずにおったら六日は出勤で、おそらく八丁堀辺りで原爆にやられとったはず。命拾いしたよ。

実家で広島に新型爆弾が落とされたのを知って、真っ先に友人・同僚の顔が目に浮かび、居ても立ってもいられなくなり、七日に広島へ戻ることにした。でも、広島から三つ手前の海田市(かいたいち)までしか汽車は動いておらず、三時間ほど歩いて市内に入りました。驚いたのは、今まで見慣れた景色がまったく見当たらなかったこと。

産業奨励館(現・原爆ドーム)のすぐそばを流れる元安川(もとやす)には、息絶えた人が幾重にも重なり合って長い列をつくっていました。熱いのと喉(のど)の渇きで、皆が先を争って飛び込んだのです。相生橋(あいおい)近くに止まっていた二両編成の電車の中は、立ったまま死んでいる人、着ている物が服か皮膚か見分けがつかない人など、無残なありさまでした。

原子爆弾の直撃を受けた八時十五分は通勤時間帯で、電車は満員だったはず。立っていた人はつり革につかまった状態ですが、つり革は焼けて無くなっている。座席もみな焼けとるんよ。それを見た瞬間、くらーっときました。現実に、地獄を見たわけじゃから。広島は、廃墟と異臭が漂う街になっていました。

　私は直接被爆をしていませんが、原爆が落とされた翌日に爆心地近くを歩いたため、いわゆる〝入市被爆〟です。でも、当時はそんなこと知らんですよ。

　やっとの思いで勤め先にたどり着いたのは、七日の夕方頃ではなかったかと思います。倉庫は土間にゴザを敷いて、怪我人を収容する場所になっていました。十三あった倉庫のほとんどに被爆者がいて、「水をくれー、水をくれー」と叫ぶ声が、あちこちから聞こえよった。臭いも、何とも言

77　　藤井三千明／藤井和子

えんほど凄いもんでした。

私は、そこで寝泊まりしながら、治療の手伝いをしました。怪我の程度はさまざまで、意識のない人、ガラスなどの破片が背中に無数に突き刺さった人、紙のように燃え尽きた服の一部だけ身に着けている人、手足が焼けただれてくっついている人、傷口にウジ虫がうごめいている人。そういう人たちが、どんどん運ばれてきました。赤十字の看護婦（現・看護師）さんが三人ほどおって、その指示で手当てをしたのですが、リバノールという黄色い薬を湿らせたガーゼを患部に貼るぐらいしかできません。それが乾いたら、はがして新しいのを貼る。患者さんに「水が飲みたい」と訴えられても、看護婦さんに「死んでしまうから水はあげないでください」と言われていたので、あげることもできず、つらい思いをしました。

たった一口の水も飲まれずに亡くなった人たちを、大八車に積んで宇品まで押して行き、山になった死体を火葬しました。百体余り連れて行ったんかな。大八車の荷台に、横に並べて六体ぐらい積む。大きい男の人の体は、荷台からはみ出るんよね。死んどる人の体は重たいんです。

宇品まで運ぶのに、一回に五十分ほどかかりました。遺骨を持ち帰り、骨壺に納めて門の所へ名前を付けて置いとくんです。家族が来て身内の名前があったら持って帰る。なかったら、しょんぼりして帰って行く。そういう光景も見ました。来る日も来る日も、昼も夜もずっと、そんな作業が八月十五日の終戦の時まで続きました。その九日間、考えることは「とにかく早く火葬したらないけん」と、もうそれのみですわ。感覚もおかしくなっとった。

終戦を迎えてからは、沼田郡安村（現在の広島市安佐南区）の役場で物資管

79　藤井三千明／藤井和子

理の残務整理の仕事をしました。進駐軍の米兵が毎日やって来て、帳簿を見てサインして帰っていきよるんよ。残務整理が終わった一九四七年（昭和二十二年）三月、福山に戻りました。

　福山もＢ29の焼夷弾で焼け野原になっていました。仲の良かった友人もたくさん亡くなり、生きる希望はますますしぼんでくる思いでした。気力もなくなり、目標もないまま定職に就くこともできず、荒れた生活を送るようになりました。それが十年余り続いたんです。広島での、あの九日間のおかしな感覚がずーっと続きよる……。しかも、広島の原爆も免れ、福山の被害からも免れて、直接的な被害におうてないわけですよ。じゃけど、わしの場合は、入市被爆(にゅうし)(まぬか)した人でも、後遺症が出とる人が多いけぇね。ほんま何にもなくて。

　二〇一三年（平成二十五年）、私は初めて人前で被爆の体験を話しました。

十分間でしたが、その間、皆さんが黙ってわしの話に耳を傾けてくださった。

本音を言えば、あんまり話しとうない。家族にも今まであまり、戦争の話はせんかった。言えば思い出すしね。言いさえせな、思い出さんでしょ。最近はないけど、よく夢に出てきましたよ。あの、悲惨な光景が。「どうしてこんなに自分が苦しめられないけんのかな」と思うたもんね。

でも、やはりね、自分が知っとることは、全部話さないけんと思うよ。今は、拾った命を使命に変えて、なるべく体験を語っていこう思うてます。

孫にも事実を伝えたい

藤井和子

——市被爆者ということを知りました。それまで、夫からは断片的

ある時、役所から夫の経歴を確認する連絡があって、夫が入

に話を聞いていたのですが、少し年が離れているせいもあって、話を聞いてもピンとこないのよ。あまりにも元気なんで、初めの頃は夫の話をなかなか信じられませんでした。被爆直後の広島に翌日入っているのに、「体になんの影響もないの？　本当なの？」って、半信半疑よね。

 夫が被爆体験を話した時、私も聞いていましたが、家では「事実は、もっと残酷よ。子どももいたんで、そのまま伝えたらショックが大きいじゃろ」と言っていました。

 被爆者のヨレヨレになった服や、溶けた弁当箱なんかを見せないほうがいいという声もありますが、私は夫の話を聞いて、事実はきちっと教えるべきだし、「言い伝えていかな、いかんな」って思うようになりました。

小学生の孫が、ゲームで遊んでいて「殺しちゃえ」なんて平気で言うのよね。命の尊さとか、死んだら戻ってこないといった実感がないわけよ。ゲームじゃったら、すぐリセットできるから、感覚が全然違うの。
やはり、戦争の悲惨さを体験した生き証人が、語り伝えていくべきですよ。孫には「おじいちゃんは、大事な宝よ」と教えたいですね。

被爆者の生きた証しを残すには、もう時間がありません。

中村一俊(なかむらかずとし)さん

(広島市安佐南区)

私が父（中村良治）の体験を聞いたのは、大学一年生の時でした。社会学の授業で、親たちが同世代の時にどんな暮らしをしていたかを聞いてリポートを書く宿題が出て、夏休みに帰省して父に話を聞きました。父が原爆に遭っていたことは知っていましたが、その時初めて、父の苦悩やつらかったことが聞けたのです。

「感覚麻痺」と表現した父

父が被爆したのは十八歳の時で、広島駅で働いていたそうです。私と同年代の時、想像を絶する異常な体験をした父は、それをまるで他人事（ひとごと）のような口ぶりで語りました。

「当時は、感覚が麻痺（まひ）していた」という父の言葉が、すべてを物語っているかのようでした。

中村一俊

被爆した広島の街を、父は「屍を乗り越えて歩いて帰った」そうです。そんな異常な光景を受け入れ、いつしか見慣れた光景になってしまうのを、父は「感覚麻痺」と表現したのだと思います。私の臆測ですが、父は戦争それ自体を「感覚麻痺」と言いたかったのではないか、という気がしてなりません。

私が幼い頃から見ていた父は、家族を養うために懸命に働き、家での晩酌を楽しむ人といった印象が強く、叱られたこともありません。ですから被爆の話を聞いた時は、優しい父と悲惨な体験がすぐには結び付きませんでした。

父の話は心にズシンと響きましたが、何よりも目の前の父が、それを体験したという事実が信じられなかったのです。信じられないという点では、父も同じ思いだったのかもしれません。日

聞きたかったことをたくさん残して逝った父

本が勝つと皆が信じていた戦争で負けた結果、それまでの価値観が真逆になってしまった日本。十八歳で、それまで信じていたものが全部否定された父は、「感覚麻痺」という言葉で記憶の彼方に押しやるしか、生きる術がなかったのだと思います。父の優しさは、持って生まれた性格だけでなく、被爆も含めた戦争という「感覚麻痺」の時代を生きたことも影響していたに違いありません。

それ以来、私は父の被爆体験を含めた戦後の生き方に関心を持つようになったのですが、聞いてみたかったことをたくさん残して、父は二〇一四年（平成二十六年）八月に逝ってしまいました（享年八十七）。

被爆後、父はリンパ腺が腫れ、手術を受けたそうです。ただ、それが原

爆の影響かどうかは、医学上、はっきり分からなかったようです。数年前、父は爆心に近い場所で被爆したことで、原爆の後遺症として広島市に認定されました。痩せていたのにコレステロール値が異常に高く、「甲状腺がおかしい」と医者に言われたそうです。原爆症なのかどうか、因果関係がはっきりしないまま、コレステロールを抑える薬をずっと飲んでいました。

今にして思えば、父から聞き漏らしたことがたくさんあったのではないか、と悔やんでいます。被爆者として差別されなかったのかとか、戦後をどんな思いで生きてきたのかといったことです。十八歳であんな目に遭い、勤め先もなくなり、水道も風呂もないバラックに住んで、そこからどうやって身を立てて結婚したのか……。

私にとって被爆体験もさることながら、被爆者の戦後の生きざま、焦土となった広島を復興させた人々の思いを後世に残し伝えなければならない

という思いが募る日々です。
被爆者の方から直に話が聞けるのは、もう時間の問題です。明確に記憶し、語ることができる世代が日に日に少なくなっています。本当に急がないといけないだろうと思います。私も被爆二世として、父のほかにも被爆体験をした親戚がいるので、話を聞いてみたい。生きた証しを残すためにも……。

生き恥をさらしてでも
伝え残したい
私の"二重の苦しみ"。

江川政市(えがわまさいち)さん

(広島市安佐南区)

私は一九二八年（昭和三年）、島根県の匹見（現在の益田市匹見町）で生まれました。父はその八年前に食いぶちを求めて日本にやって来た韓国人で、私の韓国名は、李鐘根です。

匹見にいた頃の話は、正直あまり覚えていません。その後、これもいつ頃だったかうろ覚えですが、広島の吉和村（現在の廿日市市吉和）に家族で引っ越して来ました。創氏改名で江川政市という日本名を名乗りましたが、小学校の六年生まで過ごした吉和では「朝鮮人」と言われ、差別を受ける日々が続き、惨めで悔しい思いをしました。

広島に来たことで私は、在日韓国人ゆえの差別・偏見に加えて、被爆者という〝二重の苦しみ〟を抱えることになったのです。

韓国人を隠して就職

国民学校高等科二年生（現在の中学二年生）の時、安芸郡の坂町に引っ越し、父と一緒に三菱造船のドックを造る工事現場へ働きに出ました。工事現場の人たちは気性が荒かったのですが、在日韓国人ということでの差別は、あまり受けませんでした。

働きながら高等科を卒業した十六歳の時、国鉄（現在のJR）へ就職しようと思い立ち、それなりに勉強して合格しました。

実は、これには今だから言えることがあります。採用にあたって学校から渡された書類に、私の本籍が書いてあったのを勝手に消して国鉄に提出したのです。時代が時代なので、韓国人をおいそれと雇ってくれるところなどありません。まして国営鉄道なので、入社の条件は厳しかった。でも、私は鉄道の仕事にあこがれていたので、何としても入社したかったのです。

入社後は、周囲が韓国人と気づくことはなかったと思います。日本生まれなので日本語は流暢に話せるし、会社の寮でも普通に暮らしていました。ただ寮では、先輩によく殴られました。「根性入れちゃる」という具合でね。毎晩続くんですよ、それが。

同期入社の二人は逃げ出し、実家に帰ってしまった。私もそうしたかったけど、できなかったんですよ。そこで辛抱し、ようやく寮を出て実家から通えるようになりました。

その頃、実家は廿日市の平良に移っていました。廿日市駅と広島駅を通勤往復する日々でした。職場は第一機関区といって、そこには下関や岡山などに軍事物資を運ぶ機関車を修理する機関庫があったんです。当時は広島駅のゼロ番線ホームから宇品港まで線路がありました。今でもそこには、当時の面影がわずかに残っとるように思います。

汽車に乗り遅れて生き延びた

一九四五年（昭和二十年）八月六日、その日の朝も出勤の準備をしていました。ところが、どんな理由だったか覚えていませんが、母と口論になって家を出るのが遅くなり、いつもの汽車に乗り遅れたのです。結果的に、このことで私の命は救われたと、感謝しているんです。

人類史上初めて人間に対して原爆が落とされた八時十五分。その時、私は的場の電停（路面電車）で降車し、荒神橋（爆心地から約一・九キロ）を渡っていました。もう十分遅く通過していたら、私は丸焦げになって死んでいました。突然、ピカーッという光に包まれました。八月の朝だったので太陽の光がギラギラ照りつけ、家の屋根や壁に反射しています。その上から、もうひとつ薄黄色い光が乗っかかったという感じで。この光

「普通じゃなかった」のを今でも覚えています。雷の光とは違います。あんな一瞬じゃない。「あれなんじゃろうなあ」って考える二、三秒の間があったと思います。そして「これはただ事じゃない」と思いました。すぐ弁当箱を手放し、眼鏡を外し、目と鼻と耳を押さえるような体勢で、その場に伏せました。爆弾が近くに落ちたらそうするようにと、学校や職場で訓練されていたのです。

　しばらくして、おそるおそる目を開けてみると、辺り一帯が闇でした。伏せたまま、闇に目が慣れるのを待ちました。次第に視界が開けてくると、私は目を疑いました。建物が、すっかりなくなっていたからです。それは、信じ難い光景でした。

　そして、次にとった私の行動は弁当箱探しでした。人間って、理解できないことが起きると、そこから逃れようとするんですね。薄明かりの中、

「助けてくれ」という声を背に…

あちこちまさぐりながら、二、三十メートルほど先に飛ばされた弁当箱を見つけた時、ちょっと安堵しました。

その後は、行くところなんて見当たらないし、思いつきません。ふと見ると、橋の下に避難できそうなスペースがあって、そこに移動しました。そこには先に避難していた人たちがいて、「こりゃ新型爆弾じゃ」と言っていました。ある人が私の顔を見るなり「顔が赤うなっとる」と言いました。そこで初めて自分の顔を触って「痛い」と思ったのです。いや、もしかしたら「痛い」と思ったけど実際に痛みを感じていたかどうかは、分かりません。閃光の熱線や爆風で、火傷をしていたんです。

私はそこから機関庫の方角目指して、歩き出しました。道すがら、家

の下敷きになった人がいました。「この（建物の）下に子どもがおるんです。助けてください」と叫んでいました。「助けてくれ」の声を背に受けながら、知らん顔して走り去ったんですよ、私は。その時のことを思い出すたびに「なぜ一人だけでもええけん、手を引っ張って助けんかったんじゃろうか」と。今でも消えることのない、心の葛藤です。

機関庫に到着すると、同僚たちも口々に「江川、お前、顔が赤いがな」と言います。彼らは屋内にいたので、火傷は免れていました。「火傷には油がええ」と言って、機関車の軸に注すオイルを顔や手に塗ってくれました。でもね、火傷をしたところにオイルを塗ると、飛び上がるほど痛いんですよ。機械油じゃけん、無茶な話ですよ。

夕方四時頃、鉄道社員の帽子を探そうと思って出掛けました。東練兵場を通りかかって、びっくりしました。私は国鉄の社員ですからね、制服は

しっかりちゃんとしたものなんですよ。でも、他の人は、シャツ一枚が普通、季節的にもね。そうして被爆した人が、練兵場に集まっとった。皆、真っ黒くなって。まるで炭の塊（かたまり）のように見えたんです。女性じゃろうが、もう皆が半裸状態。皮膚は腫（は）れ上がって、ただれとるし、とても人間には見えんかったです。まさに、生き地獄のようでした。

被爆から約八時間たっとるわけです。私にも、ものすごい水ぶくれが左足の後ろにできました。

「はよ死ね」と言った母の悲痛な叫び

結局、帽子は見つからず、実家がある平良までは歩いて帰りました。市内は、まだ火が残っとる状態ですよ。広島大学を通った時に、衝撃的なものを見ました。馬が死んどるんです、大きな馬が。それも目ん玉が飛

び出して。途中まで一緒に帰った仲間とおびえ上がったのを覚えています。人間の死体の山もありました。死体を見ても、何にも感じなくなっていった。でも、平常心を失った人間って怖いですよね。死体をまたぐのにも抵抗がなくなり、しまいには手足を踏みつけても罪悪感を抱かなくなりました。

橋のたもとでは、人が群がって来ました。「水をください」と言って……。それに、私たちの顔をじーっと見詰める人もいました。「助けてください」と訴えから、家族じゃないかと思ったんでしょうね。もしかしたけるようなまなざしが、今も忘れられません。

実家に帰ったのは、夜中の十二時を過ぎたころじゃったかな。家に入ると父と母がいない。弟にゆくえを聞いたら「お兄ちゃんを探しに市内に行った」と言うじゃないですか。私はね、両親には職場の住所を教えてな

かったんですよ。日本語に訛りがある父や母が職場に来ると、韓国人とばれるので、それを恐れたんです。

母は火傷だらけの人たちを見て、恐ろしくなって先に進むことができず、夜明け前に家に帰って来ました。私が家におったもんじゃから、びっくりして、わんわん泣きながら抱きしめられました。それから火傷の水ぶくれに針を刺して水を抜いてくれたり、赤チンを塗ってくれました。父は駅まで私を探しに行き、翌日の昼過ぎに帰って来ました。

火傷した皮膚は時間がたつにつれて、かさぶたができ、それをはがしながら、毎日赤チンを塗ってくれました。体の後ろは、母がやってくれました。しばらくすると、うみがたまり、そこにウジ虫が湧くようになりました。最初は母がウジ虫を取ってくれていたんですが、あとからあとから出てきます。

そのうち母が枕元に来ては、「はよ死ねやって、はよ死んでくれ」と言

うようになりました。きっと、火傷だらけの顔と体で、この先、生きていても私がつらいだけじゃろうから、と思ったんでしょうね。毎日のように、枕元で泣きながらそう言っていました。

戦争の悲惨さを忘れてほしくない

終戦後、半年ほどして、職場に通い出しました。そして一年ほどたって、「江川さん、新しい戸籍謄本を提出してください」と言われました。「分かりました」と返事をしたものの、入社時に国籍を消した書類を提出したことがばれてしまいます。もし、そんなことが発覚すると即刻クビです。それを機に、私は次第に職場から足が遠のき、しまいには退職届も出さずに辞めました。

その後は弟や妹を養うため、トラック運転手など、いろいろな職を転々

としました。父親は長い間、寝込んでいました。きっと、入市被爆のせいです。

私が、在日韓国人で被爆者という〝二重の苦しみ〟を抱えながら、しかも過去の恥を語ろうと思ったのは、戦争の悲惨さを忘れてほしくないからです。戦争で負けた国の国民が悲惨な目に遭うのは韓国の例を見ても明らかですし、勝つために手段を選ばなかったアメリカの原爆実験の犠牲者を出した日本も悲惨です。

広島平和記念公園には韓国人原爆犠牲者慰霊碑がありますが、民族的差別・偏見に苦しんだあげく、なお被爆の苦しみのなかで亡くなった同胞を思うと、私は生き恥をさらしてでも後世に伝えなければならないという気持ちになりました。

私の体験を、若い人たちが、全部でなくても、ほんの一部でも継承していっていただければ、こうして生き延びてきた意味があったと思えるのです。命の平等・無差別と、戦争の恐ろしさ、愚かさを一人でも多くの人に知ってもらえることが、私はうれしいです。

核兵器だけはいけん、と訴え続けるのが、私の使命です。

冨田照夫（とみたてるお）さん

（広島市安芸区）

「あの日」のこと

私は尋常小学校の高等科を卒業した十四歳の時に就職し、現在の安芸高田市の自宅を離れて広島市内の東雲（現在の南区東雲）の宿舎で暮らしていました。

あの日、八月六日は、朝八時の朝礼後、兵器補給所がある広島駅のホームの貨車に銃やら武器を運ぶ作業が予定されていました。その前夜は、空襲警報、警戒警報などで夜中に二度ほど起こされ、職場に向かいました。空襲警報があると、何を差し置いても職場に駆け付けるのも仕事のうちでした。そんな中での作業だったのです。

女子社員と二人で鉄砲が入った箱を提げ、「よっこいしょ」と歩みを進めた瞬間、辺り一面がピカーッと光りました。原爆投下は八時十五分です

冨田照夫

から、作業を始めた直後です。

上司の「退避中！　退避中！　退避中！」という声で退避する途中に、"誰かに突き飛ばされたような"衝撃を受け、うつぶせに地面にビターンと倒れました。うつぶせに倒れたなら、後ろからの衝撃じゃないかと思うんですが、それでも私には、どこから来た衝撃なのか、今でも定かではありません。

直後、我に返り、ほふく前進のまま、設けられていた簡易防空壕に逃げ込みました。周りの様子がどうなっていたか気になりましたが、地面とにらめっこしたまま防空壕に向かったので、直後の様子はまったく見ていません。

ただ、夕立の時のような暗さになっていたことだけは覚えています。簡易防空壕には、もう一人の男性がいて、二人入ると満員といった状態

でしたが、結局、その人とは一言も交わさないままでした。お互いに茫然自失だったんでしょうね。

そのうち壕の外が騒がしくなったので、外に出て見た光景は……。天から降ってきた「黒い雨」でした。周囲はパニックになり、「空中魚雷、空中魚雷じゃあ」という声が、どこからともなく聞こえてきました。

幽霊のような姿が

その後、先輩たちと一緒に避難しようと会社を出ましたが、いたる所でバガン、バガンと爆発音が鳴り響いていたため、怖くなって引き返しました。会社に着くと、火傷をした人がたくさん集まっていました。手の先から皮が垂れ下がり、顔はパンパンに膨らんで夢遊病者、いや、まるで幽霊のような姿でした。

107　冨田照夫

ほうっておくのも気の毒で、倉庫にムシロを敷いて寝かせました。「水をくれー」と言われても、助かりそうもない人には、あげませんでした……。それは、今見たら、とても気を保てんほど凄惨な光景でした。

私は、その夜から八月十五日（終戦の日）まで会社に居続けました。その間は上司の命令で比治山に向かい、武器を保管するトンネルの掘削作業の手伝いをしていました。車の中や倉庫の二階で寝て、全壊を免れた食堂に備蓄してあった食料で命をつないだのでした。

あの朝、一緒に箱を提げた女子社員とは、その後、再会することはありませんでした。

後遺症への不安は続く

八月十五日、上司に「ラジオのあるとこに集まれ」と言われました。そ

こで、日本の敗戦を知ったのです。その時は「まさか負けるたぁ思わんかった」というのが、正直な感想でした。そして八月三十一日まで残務整理をし、九月に入って現在の安芸高田市の実家に帰りました。

私の安否を確かめるために、原爆投下から二日ほど経って両親は広島市内に出掛ける決心をしたそうですが、たまたま地元から通っていた私の同僚が無事を教えてくれたおかげで、両親の入市被爆は避けられました。実家で久しぶりに布団で安眠した翌朝、愕然としました。枕に髪の毛がびっしりと付いていたからです。それまで寝床ともいえないような場所で寝泊まりしていたので、異変に気付くのが遅かったのでしょう。当時は原爆との関連性も分からず、「なんで抜けたんじゃろう」と不思議に思っていました。

母親が煎じてくれたドクダミ草のお茶を毎日飲んでいたら、半年後に脱

毛が治まりました。

戦後、実家で農業を手伝っていましたが、十九歳で左官の師匠に弟子入りするため、五年ぶりに広島市の土を踏みました。やがて広島で結婚し、息子たちが生まれました。原爆の後遺症らしきものも出ず、被爆者ということでの差別や偏見も受けませんでしたが、今でも「がんになるんじゃないか」とがん検診に行くたびに不安が募ります。

使命感を支えに語る

「戦争は、原爆は、おえん(いけない)。あんな悲惨は繰り返しちゃいけん」。私は被爆体験を話す時、火傷(やけど)して垂れ下がった皮を引きずりながら歩いていた人たちの姿を思い浮かべ、あの凄惨(せいさん)な光景をどう表現したらいいの

110

か戸惑いをおぼえます。

でも、それを語らないと原爆の恐ろしさを伝えることはできません。私には同い年の甥がおりましたが、学徒動員中に被爆して亡くなりました。甥がいたという場所に行くと、服の切れ端らしきものしか残っていませんでした。今でも毎年八月六日、平和公園を訪れ、甥や戦争の犠牲になった方々を悼みます。

実は、一時期、被爆体験をまったく語らなくなった期間があります。私の体験を聞いた、ある人の「あんたの話は、自分が被爆者じゃあ言うて、自慢しとるだけじゃがな」という発言がきっかけでした。それを思うと、今でも悲しい気持ちになります。

今は、「戦争の実相を伝えなければ」という私なりの使命感を支えに、口下手ながら体験を語れるようになりました。

冨田照夫

「核兵器だけはいけん」。このことは、絶対に伝えなければならないと思っています。

むすびにかえて

 被爆七十年の本年、『家族から見た「8・6」――語り継ぎたい10の証言』を発刊する運びとなりました。本書は、被爆者だけでなく、そのご家族にもお話をうかがい、その思いを掘り下げ、後世に被爆者の体験を残していくとともに、家族としてのご苦労や今後の思いを語っていただきました。

 私たちは日頃から、被爆者の方々の思いを無駄にしないためにも、「生の声」を聞いていきたいと思っています。しかし、被爆者の皆さんは、当時、家族や友人を失ったり、助けることができなかった「心の傷」を負っており、被爆体験を語ることは大変勇気がいることです。その〝勇気の言

葉〟を私たち青年が伝承者となり、語り伝えていかなければいけないと決意しました。

創価学会青年部は、「SOKAグローバルアクション」として、

①平和の文化建設・核兵器廃絶
②アジアの友好
③東北の復興

という三つの柱で平和運動を展開しております。

二〇一四年から、全国各地をはじめ、中国地方の五県でも「平和の誓いフォーラム」（被爆体験を聞く会）を開催し、青年が平和への誓いを継承しております。山口で開催したフォーラムでは、被団協（日本原水爆被害者団体協議会）の方が被爆体験を語ってくださいました。終了後、被団協の方から

「小学校や中学校等で話しをする機会はあっても、皆さんのような世代に語る機会はこれまでなかったので、ぜひ今後もお願いしたい」とのお話をうかがいました。

昨年の夏には、中国創価学会として、核兵器廃絶を求める百五十六万(全国五百十二万)もの署名を集めました。これからも、私たち二十代、三十代の青年が直接、被爆体験を聞き、不戦そして核兵器廃絶への誓いを立て、語り継いでまいります。

本年七月十九日には、広島市の広島グリーンアリーナで中国地方の五県から約八千人の青年が集い「世界青年平和音楽祭」を開催しました。中国青年部として被爆八十年までの十年間を、「核兵器廃絶へ 挑戦の10年」と決め、新たなる前進を開始しました。一人一人が平和建設への主体者として、平和の歌声を「平和原点の地・広島」から響き渡らせ、また、中国

からの留学生とともに、平和の連帯を広げるべく、日中の学生で「アジアの友好」を誓い合いました。

　池田大作SGI（創価学会インタナショナル）会長は本年の第四十回「SGIの日」に、「人道の世紀へ　誓いの連帯」と題する提言を発表しました。
　SGI会長はかねてより、被爆七十年の二〇一五年に広島や長崎で核廃絶サミットの開催を訴えてきました。これが具体化し、八月二十八～三十日に広島市内で世界のNGO（非政府組織）と連帯し、「核兵器廃絶のための世界青年サミット」を開催しました。世界の青年が被爆地・広島で一堂に会し、青年の連帯をさらに強めることができました。

　さらに、池田SGI会長は提言の中で、「四十年前の一月二十六日、グアムでSGIが発足した時、私の胸に去来していたのは〝地球上から悲惨

の二字をなくしたい"との戸田城聖第二代会長の熱願であり、『地球民族主義』のビジョンでした」と述べています。
　私たちは世界の青年と手を取り合い、そして被爆者やご家族の意思を継承し、この地球上から核兵器がなくなるよう、誓いの連帯を広げてまいります。

　　二〇一五年十月

　　　　　　　創価学会中国青年部長　守安佑介
　　　　　　　創価学会広島青年部長　高橋丈夫

solidarity for ridding the earth of nuclear weapons.

October 2015

Yusuke Moriyasu
Chief of Chugoku Youth Division of Soka Gakkai

Takeo Takahashi
Chief of Hiroshima Youth Division
of Soka Gakkai

Ikeda issued his 2015 peace proposal: "A Shared Pledge for a More Humane Future." For years President Ikeda had been calling for a nuclear abolition summit to be held in Hiroshima and Nagasaki in 2015, on the 70th anniversary of the bombings—and his wish became reality. From August 28 to 30 in Hiroshima, SGI members bonded with NGO members from many nations in the International Youth Summit for the Abolition of Nuclear Weapons. From the far corners of the world, youth gathered in a single hall to deepen their ties.

I was moved by President Ikeda's words: "On January 26, 40 years ago, when SGI was born on Guam, what struck my heart was the passionate plea of Mr. Josei Toda, the second president of Soka Gakkai: 'I want to erase the word *catastrophe* from the Earth.' I accepted as my own his vision of a global nationalism."

We want to join hands with other youths and inherit the will of the *hibakusha* and their families. We resolve to widen ever further the circles of

Gakkai collected 1,560,000 signatures on a petition demanding the abolition of nuclear weapons. (Nationwide, we collected 5,120,000.) We are in our twenties and thirties, but as we listen to *hibakusha* stories, we vow to reject war, eliminate nuclear weapons, and tell the stories we hear to others.

On July 19 of this year, roughly 8,000 young people from the Chugoku Region attended the International Music Festival for Peace by Youth at Hiroshima Green Arena. Designating the ten years between 2015 and 2025 "the Ten-year Challenge – Nuclear Abolition," the Chugoku Youth Division is developing new initiatives. After each of us vowed to become leaders in constructing peace, our songs of peace rang out from "Hiroshima—the starting point of peace." Then, Japanese students joined exchange students from China to "strengthen ties of friendship in Asia through cultural exchanges." Our goal is to widen the circles of solidarity for peace.

On the 40th "Day for SGI," SGI President Daisaku

Division has been developing three peace initiatives:

1. Advance the culture of peace and the abolition of nuclear weapons.
2. Strengthen ties of friendship within Asia through cultural exchange.
3. Continue promoting reconstruction following the Great East Japan Earthquake.

Since 2014, we have been holding "Vow for Peace" forums in which *Hibakusha* share their experiences with youth from around Japan, including the five prefectures in the Chugoku Region. These forums are encouraging many young people to inherit from our elders the peace vow. At a forum in Yamaguchi Prefecture, members of Hidankyo shared their A-bomb experiences. After it ended, one of the Hidankyo *hibakusha* said, "Even though I've spoken at elementary and junior high schools, I've not had the chance to speak to members of your generation. Please invite me again."

    Last summer, Chugoku (West Japan) Soka

In Closing

Seventy years after the atomic bombing, we are publishing "*Families Look at August 6 — Ten Accounts to Pass Forward.*" When we visited the hibakusha to hear their stories, we were often able to interview family members as well. They were willing to open their hearts and honor us by sharing their own desire to pass on the experiences of the *hibakusha*, the burdens they have borne as family members, and their hopes for the future.

That their voices may not be wasted, we will continue to make opportunities for youth to hear the *hibakusha* in person. We understand that those who bear the emotional wounds of failing to save family members and friends need great courage to share their experiences. We young people resolve to receive the stories that took such courage to share and pass them on to others.

As SOKA Global Action, the Soka Gakkai Youth

bombing while working as a mobilized student. I went to where he had been working and found only scraps of his clothing. Every year on August 6th, I visit Peace Park and mourn for my nephew and the other victims.

To tell the truth, I once stopped talking about my A-bomb experience for a while. Someone who heard my experience said, "You're just using your experience as a survivor to boast." That caused me to stop, and I feel sad about it even now. However, I am supported by my sense of mission. I feel I just have to tell the truth about war. I am not a good speaker, but I am able to tell my experience because I feel I must.

"No matter what, nuclear weapons are wrong." I absolutely have to keep saying this to the world.

hair loss stopped after six months.

I helped my parents with the farm work, but when I was 19, I stepped on Hiroshima soil for the first time in five years to be apprenticed to a master plasterer. I got married in Hiroshima; we had our sons there. I got no aftereffects from my exposure. I suffered no discrimination or prejudice as a survivor, but even now, every time I go for my regular cancer exam my anxiety level rises. "What if I have cancer?"

I speak from a sense of mission

"War is wrong. The atomic bombing was wrong. We must never repeat such a tragedy."

When I talk about my A-bomb experience, I draw pictures of the burnt victims walking along with their skin hanging down. I feel lost wondering how I can describe such a gruesome sight. But if I don't talk about it, I can't relate the horror of atomic bomb.

I had a nephew my own age. He was killed by the

Families Look at August 6, 1945

Anxiety over aftereffects never ends

Our supervisor said, on August 15th, "Go gather around the radio." It was then I found out that Japan had lost the war. It had honestly never occurred to me that we would lose the war. I stayed until August 31 to clear up some remaining tasks, then went home to Aki Takata in September.

My parents were getting ready to go to Hiroshima to look for me two days after the bombing, but a colleague who happened to commute from Aki Takata told them I was safe. Thanks to him, they were able to avoid entry exposure.

At home the morning after my first good sleep on futon in a long time, I was shocked. My pillow was covered with hair. Because I had been sleeping in places I couldn't call a bed, I had not been aware of this phenomenon. I had no idea about the effects of the atomic bombing, so I just wondered in amazement why my hair was falling out. I drank dokudami tea my mother made every day, and the

Looked like sleepwalkers

Later I fled with older workers away from the station, but explosions rang out everywhere so we grew frightened and returned to the plant. By the time we got back, many injured people had gathered. Their skin hung from the tips of their fingers, and their faces were swollen like balloons. They looked like sleepwalkers, no, more like ghosts. We couldn't just leave them, so we spread straw mats from the warehouse and laid them down. Some said "Give me water." But we didn't give water to those we thought likely to die. Thinking back on that now, I regret it, but the whole scene was so cruel.

I stayed at the plant until August 15th. During that time I was ordered by my supervisor to go up to Hijiyama Hill to help dig a tunnel to hide weapons in. I slept in a car or the second floor of the warehouse. I stayed alive eating food stored in a dining room that had escaped total destruction.

I never again saw the female worker with whom I carried the box that morning.

was as if someone had knocked me down. I fell face down on the ground with a thud. Because I fell on my face, I assume the impact came from behind me, but even now, I really don't know where that impact came from.

I came to quickly. Crawling forward, I took refuge in a temporary shelter. I was anxious about what had happened, but I just gazed at the ground as I headed for the shelter. I didn't see our general situation at all. I do remember it was dark, like during an evening shower.

Another man was in the temporary shelter, and the two of us filled it. We didn't exchange a single word. I guess both of us were stunned, out of control.

Meanwhile, I started hearing noise outside the shelter. I went outside and saw black rain falling from the sky. People around me seemed to panic. Someone said, "Sky torpedo. It was a sky torpedo!"

That day

I got a job when I graduated post-elementary school at 14. I left home in Aki Takata City to live in a dormitory in Shinonome (now, Shinonome, Minami-ku) in Hiroshima City.

On August 6th, after morning assembly at 8:00, I was scheduled to carry guns and other arms to a freight car waiting at a platform in the station where the ordnance workshop was located. I woke up twice the previous night because of an air-raid warning and a yellow alert. Each time I headed to work. Whenever an air-raid warning sounded, I had to run to my workplace immediately.

I was working with a female worker lifting up a box of guns. We grunted as we lifted it up, and we were just stepping forward when a dazzling flash filled the air. The atomic bomb exploded at 8:15, so it was right after we started working. Our supervisor shouted, "Take cover! Take cover! Take cover!" We were on our way to the shelter when I felt a shock. It

Families Look at August 6, 1945

My mission is to keep telling people that nuclear weapons are wrong, no matter what.

Teruo Tomita

(Aki Takata City, Hiroshima Prefecture)

killed by the atomic bombing, I feel I have to pass my story on to future generations, even if I have to live on in shame.

I hope young people will learn from my experience, at least part of it, so I can feel I survived like this for a purpose.

If they discovered such a fraud, I would be fired immediately. That fear gradually made me reluctant to go to work. In the end, I quit the company without sending a letter of resignation.

After that, I did many different jobs, including truck driver, in order to support my younger brother and sister. My father was bedridden for a long time. I believe it was because he was exposed to radiation while looking for me in Hiroshima.

Despite having the "double suffering" of being Korean in Japan and an A-bomb survivor, I decided to talk about my past shame because I don't want people to forget the misery of war. Any people who lose a war suffer miserably. Look at Korea, after losing to Japan. Then look at Japan, after being the victims of atomic bombs by the US, determined to win the war by any means necessary.

The Monument in Memory of the Korean Victims of the A-bomb in Hiroshima stands in Peace Memorial Park. Thinking of my fellow Koreans, who suffered terrible racial discrimination then were

to the station to look for me and came home the next afternoon.

After a while, my burnt skin scabbed over. I peeled the scabs off and applied Mercurochrome every day. My mother took care of my back. When pus began oozing out, my wounds were soon infested with maggots. At first my mother picked them all out, but they were endless.

My mother started telling me, "Hurry up and die. Please, die quickly." I'm sure she thought that with my terribly burned face and body, I would have a miserable life even if I lived. She kept saying things like that every day, crying as she did

I don't want anyone to forget the tragedy of war

About six months after the war ended I went back to work. After about a year, I received a request. "Mr. Egawa, please submit a new family register." I said, "OK." But that would reveal that I had submitted a document from which I had erased my nationality.

right over a dead body on the road. Eventually, I didn't even feel guilty stepping on their hands or feet.

People swarmed around the foot of the bridge. Some said, "Please give me water." Some gazed intently right into our eyes. Maybe they thought we were family members. I will never forget the way they looked at us as if to say, "Please save me."

It was probably after midnight when I arrived home. I entered the house, but my parents were gone. I asked my younger brother where they were. He said, "They went to Hiroshima to look for you." I had never told my parents where I worked. I was afraid if my parents showed up at work with their Korean accents, the Japanese would know I was Korean.

My mother saw terribly burned people and was frightened, unable to keep going. She came home just before dawn. She was surprised to see me already home. She squeezed me, sobbing loudly. She stuck a needle into my blisters and discharged the liquid. She applied Mercurochrome. My father went

National Railways employee, my uniform was clean and strong. But others wore shirts that were normal for the season. People that had been exposed to the bombing had gathered in the drill ground. They were all blackish and looked like lumps of charcoal. Even the women were half naked. Their skin was swollen and sore. They didn't look like human beings at all.

About eight hours after the bombing, I found I had an incredible blister on the back of my left foot.

My mother's heart-rending cry, "Die quick!"

I couldn't find my cap so I walked back to Hera where my house was. Fire was still smoldering all through the city. Walking by Hiroshima University I saw another shocking sight. A dead horse. A big horse. It's eyes were popped out. A fellow worker went part way home with me, and we were very scared. There were mountains of dead human bodies. A human being who has lost his normal mind is quite frightening, right? I came to feel nothing for dead bodies. I lost all resistance to simply walking

I started to walk toward the locomotive depot. On the way I saw someone trapped under a collapsed house. A mother was crying, "My child is under this building! Please help us!" I heard her "Help us!" behind my back, but I just kept going, pretending I didn't hear her. Every time I recall this, I get angry at myself. "Why didn't I help? I should have at least tried to pull out one child." This is an emotional conflict that will never be gone from my mind.

When I arrived at the locomotive depot, my colleagues said, "Egawa! Your face is burned." They had been inside the building so they didn't get burned. Saying, "Oil is good for burns," they put oil for locomotive engine shafts on my face and hands. But that oil on my burns was so extremely painful I jumped into the air. It was machine oil. That was crazy.

Around four in the afternoon I went out to look for my company cap, part of my uniform. Passing the Eastern Drill Ground I was shocked. Because I was a

darkness. I just lay there waiting until my eyes got used to the dark. As my sight gradually returned, I doubted my eyes. Whole buildings had completely disappeared. The scene was unbelievable.

My next action was to look for my lunch box. When something beyond comprehension happens, human beings turn their attention to something ordinary. I groped here and there in the dim light, and when I found my lunch box, which had flown twenty or thirty meters away, I felt a bit relieved.

A cry for help from behind

I didn't know where to go. I couldn't think of any place to head for. I looked around casually and found a space under a bridge. I went in. Some people who had taken refuge there before me were saying, "It's a new kind of bomb." Someone saw my face and said, "Your face is really red!" Then, for the first time I touched my face and felt pain. Or, maybe I just said, "It hurts." I don't know if I really felt pain or not. I had been burned by the flash.

cause, but I had a quarrel with my mother. I left home late and missed the train I usually got on. That quarrel saved my life, and I'm grateful.

The atomic bomb was dropped at 8:15 just as I was getting off a streetcar at Matoba and was crossing Kojin Bridge, 1.9 kilometers from the hypocenter. All of a sudden I was enveloped by a brilliant flash. That August morning, the sun was already glaring off roofs and walls. The flash looked like another ray of yellow sunlight coming in on top of the glare. I still remember how unusual that light was. It was different from lightning. It wasn't that fast. I think it lasted two or three seconds, long enough for me to think, "What is that?" And, "This isn't normal."

I dropped my lunch box, took off my glasses and threw myself onto the ground covering my eyes, nose and ears. I had been trained in school and at work to do that if a bomb fell close by.

The blast came, and after a while, I opened my eyes carefully and fearfully. The whole world was in frequently. They said, "We'll harden your spirit." And they did so every night. Two co-workers who joined the company with me ran away and went home. I wanted to quit, too, but I couldn't. I endured the beatings and finally left the dorm to commute from my house.

Around that time my family moved to Hera, Hatsukaichi. I went back and forth between Hatsukaichi and Hiroshima day after day. My workplace was the First Locomotive Yard, The locomotive depot was mainly for engines that transported military supplies to Shimonoseki and Okayama. People nowadays probably don't know that during the war we had railroad track from Hiroshima Station to Ujina Port. The trains left from Platform Zero. I think scant traces of that track and platform can still be seen.

Alive because I missed a train

In the morning on August 6th, 1945, I was preparing to go out for work. I don't remember the

the second year of junior high school. I went to work with my father at a construction site to build a dock for Mitsubishi Shipyard. Construction workers were hooligans, but they didn't discriminate against me because I was a Korean. I graduated from school when I was 16; I was still working there. I decided to get a job at Japan National Railways (now, JR). I studied hard and passed the examination.

I am able to admit something now. In the job application I was given by the school, someone had already entered my address and nationality. I erased and changed it before submitting the application to the National Railways. Hardly any companies in Japan would hire Koreans in those days, and the government-owned railways were particularly strict. But I loved the railway and desperately wanted that job.

Once I was in the company, no one noticed that I was Korean. I was born in Japan so I spoke Japanese fluently. I lived like a normal Japanese in the dormitory. Still, I was beaten by senior workers

I was born in Hikimi, Shimane Prefecture (now, Hikimi-machi, Masuda City) in 1928. My father was a Korean who came to Japan to make money eight years before I was born. My Korean name was Lee Jong Gun.

I honestly don't have much memory of Hikimi. I also don't remember much about my family moving to Yoshiwa-mura (now, Yoshiwa, Hatsukaichi City) in Hiroshima Prefecture. When we were forced to change our Korean names to Japanese, my name became Masaichi Egawa. I lived in Yoshiwa until the 6th grade. I was routinely called "Korean" (as an epithet) and was discriminated against continually. I was miserable and suffered many bitter disappointments.

Because of our move to Hiroshima City, in addition to discrimination as a Korean, I had "double suffering" after becoming an atomic bomb survivor.

Hiding my nationality to get a job

We moved to Saka-machi, Aki-gun when I was in

Families Look at August 6, 1945

I reveal my "double suffering" even if I live in shame.

Masaichi Egawa

(Asaminami-ku, Hiroshima City)

so many things. Was he discriminated against as a survivor? How was his feeling during that post-war time. He encountered such a terrible thing when he was 18. He lost his job. He lived in a hut with no water and no bath. How did he rebuild his status in society and get married from there. I take the A-bomb experience for granted, in a way, but day by day I feel more strongly that I have to pass on to future generations the way survivors lived after the war and the thoughts and feelings of the people who rebuilt Hiroshima from that plain of burnt ruins.

It's a matter of time before the chance to hear in person the stories of survivors is gone. The generation that remembers that experience clearly and can share it with others is dwindling. We need to hurry. As a second-generation survivor, I want to hear the experiences of other relatives. I want to create and leave proof that they lived.

through that time of "sensory paralysis," including both the war and the atomic bombing.

My father was gone before I asked

I became interested in how he lived from the time of the bombing through the post-war turmoil, but he passed away in August 2014 at the age of 87 leaving me with a lot of questions I wanted to ask.

After the bombing he developed swollen lymph glands and underwent an operation. Whether or not it was an effect of the bombing was medically unclear. Several years ago, because he was exposed fairly near the hypocenter, he was officially recognized as a survivor by the City of Hiroshima. His cholesterol was abnormally high despite being thin, and a doctor once told him, "Your thyroid is strange." He took medicine to control his cholesterol for a long time, again not knowing whether it was atomic bomb disease or not.

Thinking back now I regret that I failed to ask him

was calling the war itself a time of "sensory paralysis."

I have known my father all my life. When I was a child, he worked hard to raise his family, but he enjoyed a drink with dinner at home. He never once scolded me. Therefore, when I heard his A-bomb story, I couldn't quite relate my gentle father to his tragic experience. What he told me laid heavy on my mind, but more than anything, I could not believe that the man before my eyes, my father, had experienced such things.

It may be that he himself found his experience impossible to believe. When Japan lost the war he had been convinced it would win, the whole world turned upside down. His values were suddenly reversed. At the age of 18, everything he had thought right suddenly turned out to be wrong. To survive, he had no choice but to push aside his war experience and call the whole thing "sensory paralysis".

His gentleness was part of his nature. He was born with it, but it was also affected by having lived

I was a first-year student at university when I heard my father's experience. His name was Yoshiharu Nakamura. I had a social studies assignment to interview my parents about the lives they had lived and write a report. I came home during summer vacation and heard my father's story. I had known he was in the atomic bombing but this was the first time I heard details about his pain and suffering.

That day was "sensory paralysis."

My father was 18. He was working in the Hiroshima station. He had an extraordinary experience, far beyond my imagination, when he was my age (at the time we talked), but he spoke as if it had happened to someone else. I understood why when he said, "My senses were numb then." This made a powerful impression on me; it explained everything.

He "walked home stepping over dead bodies." He used the term "sensory paralysis" to express his ability to accept such surreal scenes as normal without realizing what he was doing. My guess is he

Families Look at August 6, 1945

No time left to leave proof the survivors ever lived.

 **Kazutoshi Nakamura**

(Asaminami-ku, Hiroshima City)

life or the fact that a living creature dies and never comes back. He plays games he can reset easily. His consciousness is completely different.

Living witnesses who experienced the misery of war must hand down their stories. I want to tell my grandchild, "Your grandpa is a treasure."

contacted me to confirm my husband's personal history. That is how I came to know he was an entry survivor. Until then I had heard fragments of his story but, partly because our ages are different, I couldn't quite comprehend what he said. He was unbelievably healthy, so I couldn't accept his story at first. He entered Hiroshima right after the bombing, the next day. "You had no aftereffects? Really?" I couldn't help being doubtful.

When my husband shared his A-bomb experience I listened to his public talk. Then, at home he said, "It was actually far, far worse than that. There were children in the audience. I'm afraid they would be terribly shocked if I really told them the way it was."

Some say it's better not to show tattered clothes or charred lunchboxes, but after I heard my husband's experience I came to believe we have to teach the truth and pass the story on from generation to generation. My grandchild in elementary school plays video games and never hesitates to say, "I'll kill you!" He has no real sense of the sanctity of bombings in Fukuyama. I never suffered any obvious damage. Many entry survivors suffered aftereffects, but I have had no problem.

I talked about my atomic bomb experience for the first time in front of an audience in 2013. I spoke for only ten minutes but everyone quietly listened to my story. To be honest, I don't want to talk about it. I haven't talked about it even to my family. If I speak, I recall.

If I don't speak, I don't have to remember. It doesn't happen anymore, but I used to see the bombing in my dreams—those tragic sights. I often thought, "Why do I have to suffer so much?"

I have to tell everything I know. I have made that my life's mission, so I intend to share my experience as much as I can.

I want to tell the truth to my grandchild. (Kazuko Fujii)

One day someone from the municipal office

many such scenes. Day after day, night after night, we worked continuously until the war ended on August 15th. During those nine days my only thought was, "I have to cremate them as quickly as possible." That was the only thing in my mind. I felt so strange.

After the war I worked to tie up loose ends for supply management at the village office in Yasu-mura, Numata-gun (now, Asaminami-ku,Hirosima city). An occupying US soldier came every day to check the books, give his signature and leave. I went back to Fukuyama in March 1947, when the job of clearing things up ended.

Fukuyama had also been reduced to a burnt plain by B29 incendiary bombings. Many of my good friends were killed, and my desire to live faded. I lost my spirit. I was unable to find a job; I had no goal or direction. I started living a wild life that continued for more than ten years. The strange feelings I developed during my nine days in Hiroshima continued for all those years. I had escaped direct exposure to the bomb in Hiroshima and the

Cross Hospital, and we offered treatment according to their instructions. There was not much we could do except put gauze with a yellow antiseptic called Rivanol on the wounds. When the gauze got dry, we took it off and put on a new one. The victims kept begging, "Please, give me some water." But the nurses said, "Don't give them water; they'll die if you do." I hated not giving them water.

When they died anyway without even a sip of water, we heaped their bodies on a cart and pushed them to Ujina, where they were cremated in mountains of corpses. I'm sure we carried more than 100. We would put six bodies side by side and on top of each other in the cart. Large men would stick out over the end of the cart. Dead bodies are heavy.

It took 50 minutes to make one trip to Ujina. We brought back the ashes, put them in urns, wrote their names on the urns, which we put out on the gate. When family members found those urns, they would take them home. Those who came looking but failed to find any loved ones left looking so dejected. I saw streetcar, I felt dizzy. I knew I was looking at hell. Hiroshima lay in ruins, filled with a foul smell.

I was not exposed to the bombing directly, but I walked near the hypocenter the day after the bombing. Therefore, I'm an entry survivor. At the time, of course, I had no such idea.

I somehow managed to get to my workplace in the evening of the 7th. In the warehouse, the injured lay on mats were spread out on the earthen floor. Victims were lying in most of the 13 warehouses. Cries for water came constantly from here and there. The smell was terrible; I have no way to describe it.

I stayed there and helped to care for the victims. There were all levels of injury. Some were unconscious. Others were pierced by hundreds of glass fragments. One who had only torn rags for clothes was burned black all over like a piece of paper. Some were burned so badly their legs were fused together. Wounds were swarming with maggots. Such victims were carried in one after another. There were three nurses from the Red

I was at home when I heard a new type of bomb was dropped on Hiroshima. Immediately the faces of my friends and fellow workers appeared before my eyes. I was unable to sit still. I went back to Hiroshima on the 7th, but the train stopped at Kaitaichi, three stations before Hiroshima. I walked three hours to get to the city. I was stunned. The cityscape I knew was completely gone.

Along the Motoyasu River running past the Industrial Promotion Hall (now, the A-bomb Dome), I saw long, high piles of corpses. So many had jumped into the river due to heat, pain, and thirst. Some died standing up. Some were so burned I couldn't tell if they were wearing clothes or not.

Inside a two-car tram stopped near the Aioi Bridge I saw an especially cruel sight. The atomic bomb hit the streetcar at 8:15am.

It was morning rush hour, so the tram was full. People were still standing, as if holding onto straps, but the straps were burned away. All those sitting were burned as well. The instant I looked into that

I was an entry survivor and didn't know it. (Michiaki Fjii)

I worked for Army Clothing Depot in Hiroshima City. I took leave and went home to Fukuyama on August 6th, the day of the atomic bombing.

In our factory, about 2500 employees made shoes, shirts and other clothing for soldiers. It was quite difficult to get leave from work because of the war. I wet a stamp and peeled it off an envelope I had received some time earlier.

I wrote, "Father seriously ill; return immediately." I put the used (peeled) stamp on an envelope and made it look as if the letter was just delivered. I showed it to my boss, and he let me go home. I desperately wanted to go home so I cheated. I simply was overwhelmed by my desire to go home the day before the bombing.

I don't know what drove me like that, but if I had not gone home, I would have gone to work and probably would have been killed around Hatchobori (downtown). My desire to go home saved my life.

Families Look at August 6, 1945

The situation was so horrible, far beyond words; still, we must pass on our stories.

 **Michiaki Fujii**

 **Kazuko Fujii**

(Fukuyama City, Hiroshima Prefecture)

the war until today. I didn't tell your mother when I married her. When she found out I was a survivor she just said, "So you're a hibakusha then, right?" She had no prejudice against me. To tell the truth, her attitude saved me. I wasn't trying to hide anything from her. I just never felt I wanted or should tell her. She didn't care whether I was exposed or not. She didn't see it as a problem and had no sense of discrimination. Since my wife sees me that way, I don't care what other people think. I'm happy.

but found nothing special. I had fever of about 40 degrees Celsius for a week, but after that I got well.

My cherished desire

I don't know if it was an aftereffect of the bombing or not but my lower intestine came out, and I had an operation. I have macula lutea degeneration in my eyes. I go to a doctor in Hiroshima once every two months. I'm old, but this tells me I'm supposed to live a bit more, and I'm grateful.

Our life after the war was truly miserable. War is wrong, no matter what happens. War is no good. It's especially terrible for women. We called those who lost their husbands widows. That made me angry. No wives willingly send their husbands to the battlefield. That's why I feel so strongly that militarism is plain wrong. This is my opinion. And if Japan had won the war, Japan would be completely different from what we have today.

I haven't told anyone about the atomic bombing or

headed back toward Hiroshima. In Hiroshima, the ties on the Enko Streetcar Bridge were burning.

I was thinking I wouldn't tell you this, but a burnt military officer was on the riverbank by Enko Bridge. He ordered me to carry a wooden door. An officer's order was an absolute command at that time, so I carried the door as ordered. But when he tried to make me help him carry dead bodies, I ran away. Even the skin on the military horses was blistered. I felt sorry for them. When I got to the Enko River it was low tide so I walked to the other side.

I heard a train running from Kaita so I walked there. I was young and able to walk even though I hadn't eaten all day. The train was full. I clung to the wall of the coal car behind the locomotive and headed home.

I think I got home around 11 that night. My mother and brother said, "You smell. You're stinky." They were right, because of the burns. I had burns on my exposed skin. A doctor nearby came to see me

Tragic scenes I saw that day (Hase tsuchio)

If I had left home even a little later I would have been hit downtown in a streetcar, but I was already walking when I heard the huge boom. I fell immediately to the ground behind a ridge next to a rice field. I thought, "What was that? I wonder if they dropped some sort of light bomb."

When I cautiously looked up, I saw a grassy area already burning. The harvested rice drying in another field was also burning. I looked toward my company and saw the roof of the building completely gone. Only the iron skeleton remained. I decided not to go to work. I fled along Route 2 but felt like I was at the entrance to hell. I saw long lines of people with skin blistered and peeling off. My skin was also peeling where it was bare.

As I was walking toward Itsukaichi, to the west, it started raining, black rain. I managed to get to an elementary school. I went to a person nursing the injured, but she said, "You're young. Go away." So I

been no war, there would have been no atomic bomb. Therefore, to avoid any repetition of the tragedy of Hiroshima, Japan should never again go to war. We should never glorify any kind of war.

After talk about this with him, I finally understood why my father was always saying, "This peaceful Japan is precious. We have to take good care of this happiness.

I want to say, "Dad, there's nothing like experience, right?"

My father was exposed to the atomic bombing when he was 18. He was mobilized to work for Mitsubishi Machinery, four kilometers from the hypocenter. He went home on August 5th because it was Sunday. The next day he took a streetcar from Hiroshima Station, getting off at Kanon-machi (now, Nishi-ku,Hiroshima city). He was walking toward the company when the atomic bomb exploded.

I will put down my father's words as he told them to me.

There's nothing like experience (Tokutomo Hase)

Hearing my father, Tsuchio, tell his story, I felt that he sees the atomic bombing in a way that is quite different from the thinking of most survivors. Rather than lamenting over past, he concentrates on treasuring the happiness he enjoys now. Rather than talking about his atomic bombing experience, he wanted to tell me his antiwar sentiment. I feel sure that's because he is focused on the present.

Each survivor has a different way of thinking, and second-generation survivors have still other ways of thinking. I had eczema as a child and always wondered if it was a kind of A-bomb disease. But it subsided when I grew up. A long time has passed, so we can't say that all the illnesses of survivors and second-generation survivors are connected to the bomb. But we never know. Doctors can't tell if a disease is due to the atomic bomb or not.

One thing I can say for sure is that if there had

Families Look at August 6, 1945

I want you to know what my father said.

Tokutomo Hase

Tsuchio Hase

(Takehara City, Hiroshima Prefecture)

cancer. I'd lived free of health problems, so being a second generation survivor had not felt real to me. Now it does.

Seventy years after the bombing, I bow my head to the young persons who are becoming A-bomb storytellers to convey the experiences of survivors to coming generations. I'm not good at speaking. I lack the courage to do it myself, but it's critical that people step up to pass the stories forward.

Keeping peace requires us to strengthen our resolve never to make war. It is deeply reassuring to know that so many young people understand this.

Sachiko Nakanishi

My sister was a "Hiroshima Maiden"

My sister, who is six years older, was a "Hiroshima Maiden." There was a period when we were forced to confront the bombing even if we hated to, but mostly I lived without feeling forced to talk about it. Even when I married, I did not mention that my father had been in the bombing, that I was a second generation survivor. Now I wonder: "Was it wrong not to admit that?"

As a child, I was weak. Riding buses gave me motion sickness. Twice, I could have toured the A-bomb museum with my class, but I declined because I feared motion sickness riding the bus.

My son said, "Mother, you live in Hiroshima, but you've never been to the A-bomb museum. That's just wrong." When he was a child, he toured the museum on a class trip. When he got home, he told me, "I cried. I couldn't eat my lunch. Mom, you have to go there with me." That son is now 32 years old.

Two years ago, I underwent surgery for thyroid

entered the shell of the company building. All the glass had shattered. The doors were barely standing but the walls had crumbled, except for the posts.

Walking home, she was hit by black rain that stained her blouse black. Washing did not erase the stains.

"That was black hail, you know," Aunt Yasuko said.

This is what she had to say about her experience. "Lots of people lay where they'd fallen, their skin peeling as cleanly as a glove pulled back halfway off the hand. The roads were full of glass shards. Every evening, we smelled the stench from piles of corpses burning. We don't need any more war, that's for sure."

I was about 20 when my father spoke directly to me about his experience. I don't know where we were, but I believe we were alone when I asked him what happened. He died in 1979.

bring him back home. I don't remember him ever telling us what happened to him at the ABCC, but I vaguely understood that it had to do with illness caused by the bombing.

Every morning, my mother applied hot water to my father's lips with a piece of gauze. Some time later, my father was finally able to move his lips.

The bombing and my aunts

My father's younger sisters also were exposed to the bombing. Shizuko, who was 17, died. She had been en route to Girls School. That evening, a neighbor carried her home in a cart. Her skin was melting off, but she could still speak. Nonetheless, in the middle of the night on the 7th, she passed away.

His other sister, Yasuko, who was 20, was exposed at the company where she worked as a telephone operator. When the bomb exploded at 8:15, she was on break in the waiting room, which saved her life. At the huge roar, she jumped up and ran to the air-raid shelter. After some time, she came out and

"I was terrified." Behind my father's words I sensed anguish and despair at his powerlessness. When he got back to his company, he was given three cans of butter to apply to his burns. Then he headed home to Hatsukaichi. He was burned on his back, but his burns did not form keloids.

On the way home, he saw piteous sights, such as a mother who may or may not have known that the baby she carried on her back was dead. People were seeking water, jumping into the rivers—through this hell, he walked to Hatsukaichi. He did not arrive until the next day, August 7.

In 1950, when I was two, our family moved to Minaga, on a hill in Itsukaichi. Our house was a converted old storage building with a corrugated tin roof.

Around two years later, my father's lips began to fester. I remember the black vehicle of the ABCC (Atomic Bomb Casualty Commission) coming every Friday to our house to pick him up and later

Sachiko Nakanishi

My father's A-bomb story

My late father, Masato Watanabe, was born in Koi-machi, Hiroshima City, in 1914. After graduating from post-elementary school, he worked until around 1941 on an official government ship. Then he took a job at Tanaka Refrigeration in Koi.

When the bomb dropped, he was 32 years old. He had left his company on business and was walking near Hakushima Elementary School (now, Nishi-Hakushima-machi, Naka-ku, Hiroshima-city) when suddenly, everything was bathed in a flash. He jumped into a ditch, pressing his fingers against his ears and eyes, as he'd been trained to do in bomb drills.

Immediately after came a huge roar and blast. When he returned to consciousness, he found himself almost naked. He found a towel to cover himself and headed back toward his company. He ran into people whose skin was peeling and hanging from their fingertips.

Families Look at August 6, 1945

I want youth to strengthen their resolve never to make war.

 **Sachiko Nakanishi**

(Otake City, Hiroshima Prefecture)

parent and child. We were being careful of each other's feelings. If we delved into it, questions would come up. "Why didn't we rescue them?" "We should have gone in, even if we burned up with them." If even I, a child at the time, blamed myself with such thoughts, how much more deeply must father have felt them! All survivors bear these wounds of the heart. This is why I never talked to my son. If I did, the tears would come as I was forced to remember ...

Now we have peace. To ensure that it continues, we must convey to people the horror of war. If that awareness takes root in the youth, when the rush to war arises, they will stand up and wave the flag that says, "No war."

I countered, "What do you think it is?"

"Getting rid of the thoughts that make us want to hurt one another."

I was deeply moved, because I felt that he truly understood.

We who have experienced war believe that peace means absolute refusal to make war. This does not require reason to understand. Hibakusha don't enjoy sharing their experiences because we don't want to cry. The catastrophe was just too cruel, too horrible for words. It was a dark world utterly devoid of the light of human feelings. A living hell. We have no way to communicate this, so we remain silent. I believe that this feeling is common to all survivors.

While my father was alive, he never spoke of his experience. When I told this to another peace volunteer, she asked, "Why didn't you and your father speak of what the two of you had been through?"

We did not—we could not—because we were

mother worries about what kind of children we'll have." But he himself was sympathetic and always told me, "Don't work too hard."

I got my Atomic Bomb Survivor Health Book in 1962, when I was 19. Survivors were often hurt by the way people reacted when they learned that we'd been in the bombing. Lots of us were slow to apply for the status. I was 22 when I married. The preceding two years, I worked for Daiichi Life Insurance in Moto-machi. My father lived to be 91 without any particular ailments. I cared for him at home until the end.

Thoughts of a survivor

When I started being the Hiroshima Peace Volunteer, I guided elementary school children who came on class trips through the A-bomb museum. When we were done, they'd share their impressions with me. A sixth grade boy said, "What sticks with me is your saying, 'War makes people lose their hearts.' What do you think peace is?"

Though the building had survived, it was damaged. If it rained, we had to move bringing our desks. The roof was galvanized iron, and it let the rain through. The auditorium was a buckled and twisted iron skeleton. Together with my classmates or neighbor kids, I'd go to a concrete structure with tile floor in the ruins and play house. Whenever we dug, human bones would come up. In time we lost our repulsion or fear of human bones. Many air-raid shelters had been dug around the bottom of Hijiyama Hill, where we'd sometimes go to do group exercises to the radio. Many people were living in these shelters. Even two or three years after the bombing people were living there.

As a child, I never felt discrimination for being a hibakusha. After all, everyone around me was one. But when I wanted to marry, I hid the fact of my exposure. The go-between who arranged the marriage, however, had keloids on her hands and face. Sometime after we married, my husband asked, "Were you in the atomic bombing?" He went on, "My

After we were sufficiently recovered, my aunt, my father and I returned to Showa-machi every day to look for the remains of mother and my little brother. The first task was to identify our house within the mass of burnt ruins. All had been flattened, leaving nothing to serve as a marker. Because we had no idea where to start, father later came back alone to search. A few days later, he brought home something that he called their bones. I had no way of knowing whether that was true or not.

Because people were saying, "Nothing will grow in Hiroshima for 70 years," my father was leaning toward abandoning Showa-machi and building a little house in Fukugi-mura. But when I was in the second semester of my sixth grade year, he said, "Little by little, people are going back. Let's go back, too."

So we built a shack in the ruins of our home in Showa-machi for father, grandmother, and me. Our school was not yet rebuilt, so I went to Senda Elementary School in the neighboring district.

Life after the bomb

The next day, the Shinonome Women's Association made rice balls and handed them out. The morning after that, father and I were heading to Fukugi-mura when he said, "I can't stand up." It must have been an injury from being squeezed under the collapsed house. Then he had to walk on his knees. A truck picked us up and carried us. Finally we arrived at my grandmother's house in Fukugi.

Both Father and I came down with diarrhea and vomiting; our hair fell out. A doctor in the neighborhood said, "Could be dysentery, I don't know." We later understood that we were suffering acute effects of the bombing, but at the time we thought it might be dysentery. Lacking medicine, grandmother and my aunt went to the river to pick Saururaceous plants. We drank tea made from these plants in place of medicine. My aunt (father's younger sister) had evacuated there after losing her home in the air raids in Kure.

centigrade, igniting anything flammable.

Weaving through collapsed houses and flaming wreckage, father and I aimed ourselves at Hijiyama Hill. We were both barefoot.

The people we saw along the way had all been thrown somewhere by the bomb. Those who had been inside were trapped in the rubble and burned to death. We heard, "Help! Help me!" but they screamed to no avail. When we got to Hijiyama Bridge, we saw many people in the river, many more jumping in. When I looked carefully, I saw bodies piled on bodies, all floating in the water. People were piled up on both sides of the bridge—their skin burnt black or peeling off.

Afraid to stay there, we crossed Hijiyama Bridge and found our way to a vineyard in Shinonome-cho (now, Shinonome, Minami-ku, Hiroshima-city), four kilometers away. Many others took refuge there as well. We spent the night looking back at Hiroshima, where pillars of red flame shot up here and there.

help us. I went back and said, "Daddy, there's no one to help!" He pointed to an iron shaft nearby and said, "Bring that to me." I handed it to him, and he inserted it between the threshold and the lintel. Fighting for his life must have provided superhuman strength. Even squatting, he was able to lift the weight enough to free his arm. Then he was out.

The two of us began looking for mother and my little brother, but we had only their voices to go by. We couldn't tell where they were. Soon, flames licked up just as we stopped hearing mother's voice. Sparks landed on me and ignited my clothes. Father quickly put out the fire. Then he found a futon, doused it in the water cistern, and went into the flames holding it over him, trying to find his wife and son.

At the time, every house had a cistern in front for putting out flames in the event of bombing. But when this bomb exploded, those who were not making breakfast still had charcoal smoldering. The charcoal eventually ignited flames here and there. Apparently, the ferocious heat of the bomb shot up ground temperatures to 3,000-4,000 degrees was getting ready to return a book I had borrowed from a friend in the neighborhood. Just as I opened the sliding paper and wood doors, they fell down on me. I don't know how long I lay trapped under them. When I came to, I saw a faint light far away. I thought if I could get there, I could get outside. So I struggled through the wreckage and finally made it out.

When I was hit, I heard nothing. Later, I heard people talk about the *pika* (flash) and the *don* (roar), but inside the house, I saw nothing and heard nothing. I thought, "A bomb fell on our house!" Our two-story house completely collapsed. From somewhere underneath, my mother was calling, "Help! I'm here! Help!" I saw my father crouching, his left arm trapped between the threshold and the lintel. He could not move. Father cried, "Get someone to come help us!"

I walked around the area, but our neighbors were trapped under houses, too. People who had been exposed outside were injured. I found no one to exposed in the third grade, when I was eight. At the time, the government ordered children from the third grade to the sixth grade to evacuate to the countryside. Children went to stay with relatives if they could; otherwise, they went with their classes to stay somewhere as a group. My parents found distant relatives who were willing to take me in. I went to Fukugi-mura in Takamiya-gun (now, Higashi-ku, Hiroshima-city) and attended Taketani Elementary School. Lots of other children from Hiroshima who had evacuated with their classes were there, too. Daily necessities were hard to come by, and we kids went to school barefoot.

On the night of August 4th, 1945 my father came to pick me up and take me home for a visit before heading to my new evacuation site, my mother's family. The next night, my father and I walked the ten kilometers home to Showa-machi. We arrived during the night; I was so exhausted, I went right to sleep.

On the 6th, my parents, my five-year-old brother, and I ate breakfast and went back to our rooms. I

but we never discussed the bombing. I'm sure that she wished not to recall it.

My mother first shared her own A-bomb experience in 2007, when she began working as a "Hiroshima peace volunteer" (a guide in the Peace Memorial Museum).

But, After mother had her myocardial infarction, she could no longer work as a peace volunteer. This was so unfortunate, because the work had given her something to look forward to. But as her son, I feel glad that we found this way to preserve her experience and her thoughts against war.

What follows is the account she struggled to write, to which I've added details that she shared with me.

That day
(Michiko Katsunori)

I (=Michiko) was born in Showa-machi (now, Shouwa-machi, Naka-ku, Hiroshima-city) and was

My mother's experience and her thoughts against war
(Takashi Katsunori)

When I was a child, I wondered why my mother, Michiko's feet were cracked. Years later, she told me, "We got out of there running desperately on bare feet. . . The river was full of dead bodies." In her retelling, I felt her bravery and understood that the bombing's power to influence comes from its cruelty and inhumanity.

In January 2014, my mother had a myocardial infarction; later, she suffered multiple fractures in her back. She had four compression fractures in her spine and one in her hip. Now that she is in her 70's, her body is weak; her height has shrunk 16 centimeters.

Mother says, "Since it isn't clear whether the atomic bombing or my age is the cause, I'm not going to blame the bombing." Mother and I had argued in the past over the causes of her diseases,

Families Look at August 6, 1945

Saying, "It's for the future," Mother opened up about the past she wanted to forget

 **Takashi Katsunori**

 **Michiko Katsunori**

(Asakita-ku, Hiroshima City)

like my only keepsake from them.

When I was a child, my hair fell out easily and I frequently felt nausea. I don't know if these were effects from the bomb or not. Ten years ago, I was operated on for thyroid cancer, but I do not know if that was related or not. Since I turned 70, I easily break bones and suffer eye ailments. Various parts of my body are weakening. Maybe it is simply my age, but I often feel that my A-bomb exposure is affecting my health.

Though my sons are second-generation victims, and though people advise them to apply for the Health Book, they both refuse. They have their own ways of thinking about this that I must respect. I have had the good fortune to live with my son without any recurrence of tragedy like I suffered. These are good days, and I am happy.

In my three-page application I listed the days I thought I had entered the city and the reasons I had entered. I submitted one copy to Hiroshima Prefectural Government Office and one more for my brother-in-law to Ehime Prefectural Government Office. I needed proof that I had attended elementary school, so we asked the Board of Education of Takata Gun to search through the lists of students for my name and asked for proof of my enrollment from Imabari Elementary School. We found someone who provided witness that I had been in Hiroshima the days I indicated. My application was accepted and my Health Book was issued. My brother-in-law in Shikoku was also recognized as an entry survivor, but he died two years later. My sister who was four years older, who was rained on by black rain at my side, did not receive the Health Book because she had been officially evacuated in the group evacuations.

When I received the Health Book at age 48, I felt it was a gift from my departed parents. We had not even found their remains, so this Health Book felt (now, nagahara, hatsukaichi-city) for about two years. In Nagahara I worked all day on farms. An acquaintance introduced me to the man I married. He was working in forestry at the time, but he later joined a company. He died at age 63. We had two sons. I now live with the younger son.

At my older son's wedding, my brother-in-law in Shikoku talked to me about the time he came to get me and asked, "Tatsuko, did you get an Atomic Bomb Survivor Health Book?" The atomic bombing had happened 40 years previous when I was in the first grade. I had been hit by black rain and entered the city to look for my father's body. A week after the bombing, my brother-in-law and I walked through the city and slept outdoors at Hiroshima Station. I realized that I was an "entry survivor." I'd never applied for one because I had been healthy and because I couldn't write properly, not having graduated from school. I didn't feel I could fill out the application. But my husband said he would help me with the process, so I decided to do it.

there. We slept outside in Hiroshima Station. The next morning, we went to Onomichi and learned that the war was over.

When our brother returned from the war, he took my sister, who was four years older, and me into his home. For a year, we lived together in Shioya, Kobe. But he could not earn enough to take care of two little sisters. It was decided that one of his war buddies would take me in. So I moved to live with that family in Hitoyoshi-City, Kumamoto Prefecture.

Meanwhile, my brother worked in a mine in Yamaguchi Prefecture. There he was killed in September 1950, when the Kezia Typhoon caused a landslide that buried him. My brother survived a war, returned to find his parents and two sisters dead; entering the post-surrender climate of despair, he worked desperately hard, only to die in an accident. Whenever I think of him, my anger at war surges again.

I lived in Kumamoto until I was 18, when I moved to Hiroshima, relying on help from my aunts. I lived in Nagarekawa one month, then in Nagahara

"Is Haruji Yamakado in there? If you're in there, please get off here!" But he was not in any truck.

Later, one of the neighbors came by to say, "Haru-san died. Killed by the pika (atomic bomb)." We wept and wept. Later, we went into the city. I remember walking through the ruins with my sister holding my hand or carrying me on her back. I don't remember seeing bodies, so we must not have gone in the first day or two. Even so, a sharp smell pierced our noses. We could not find father's corpse, just as we had not found mother's.

Received A-bomb Health Book at age 48

In my first year of school, I had lost both parents, and my brother was still off at war. Now my life was being shuttled from place to place, depending on relatives and friends. First I went to Imabari in Shikoku, where my sister had gone as a bride. My brother-in-law came to get me. To get to Shikoku, we had to change trains in Hiroshima. It must have been a week after the bombing, but the stench was still

Father dies in atomic bombing

Our family's wartime tragedy was hardly over. My father, my two older sisters and I left Kobe for our mother's birth home in Yachiyo-cho, Takata-gun (now, yachiyo-cho, Akitakata-City), Hiroshima Prefecture. My oldest remaining sister soon entered the dormitory of a spinning factory in Mihara.

When the bomb fell on Hiroshima, I could feel the impact out in Yachiyo (about 30 kilometers away). Amazed, I ran out of the house and looked up to see a pitch-black cloud rising in the sky. That day (August 6th) my father had gone to Hiroshima on business. My fourth-grade sister and I were supposed to watch the house, but we feared so for our father that we had to stay outside to look for him. While we sat by the roadside, we were rained on by black rain full of ash. We had no way of knowing it was radioactive rain.

While being hit by black rain, we waited for the trucks coming from Hiroshima. Trucks came by filled with burned people. We cried out to stop them.

Through the sea of fire and smoke, we ran, trying to get to the designated neighborhood refuge.

On the way, we encountered burned people who begged, "Give me water!" Injured people could not move, but we could do nothing—saving ourselves was all we could do. When we got to the refuge and did not see mother and our other sisters, our fear grew. That night, I wailed and screamed, "Mother is dead!" which was very hard on my sister.

Two days later, my sister and I went home. The house had burned down. My sister said, "I remember what Mother was wearing," as we dug through the wreckage. All around us, people were using sticks to probe the ruins. The air was suffused with a strange smell. We never found the bodies of my mother or our sisters.

We stayed in the shelter for a week, wearing the same clothes. To assuage our hunger, we had packages of hard bread and water poured from kettles.

Tatsuko Ota

Air raids in Kobe took mother and two sisters

Our family was mother, father, and eight children. The oldest was my brother; all the rest were girls. I was the youngest. By the time I was old enough to remember things, we were at war, and my brother was gone to the front. One of my sisters was married, another had been evacuated to the countryside, and a third had been adopted by a relative. Left in our house in Nada, Kobe, were four daughters, my mother, and my father, who had retired from military service to work for a company.

I had started elementary school when the American air raids became so intense that schoolwork was abandoned. I was in the first grade on June 6th, 1945, when an air attack began at around 9 a.m., after my father left for work. Incendiary bombs thudded to the ground all around us and exploded. Bam! Bam! Around us swirled a sea of flame. I called mother—no answer. My sixth-grade sister, who was near me, grabbed my hand.

Families Look at August 6, 1945

War stole my parents and ripped apart my family—My tragedy must never be repeated

Tatsuko Ota

(Hatsukaichi City, Hiroshima Prefecture)

struggling to raise us all, I remembered the atomic bombing. They were the main victims. My mother died of cancer at 74.

After the surrender, my father worked in Hiroshima. He died of old age at 92. I don't think our family suffered prejudice because we were *hibakusha*.

I was angry, really bitter about the bombing, but I let those feelings go.

Families Look at August 6, 1945

My brother Fu-chan, exposed in the womb

My mother worried about my burns something awful, but compared to what happened to others, mine were light. I was burned from the back of my head down to my neck and upper back. I was wearing glasses, and it was summer. When I sweat, the burned skin under the glasses hurt. Then that got infected and hurt more. It took a long time to heal.

There was a bank next to the Chugoku Shimbun (the local newspaper company) in Kaminagarekawa-cho (now, Ebisu-cho, Naka-ku). They turned the roof into a first-aid station. I went there for treatment for days. Years later, I got prostate cancer, but the doc said it wasn't related to the atomic bombing.

At the time of the bombing, our household was my parents and four kids. But mother was pregnant. My little brother Fumio (Fu-chan) was born after the war. He was exposed in the womb, and his brain was affected by Down's syndrome. Whenever I saw my little brother, so far from me in age, and my mom

some. No one died immediately, but some looked so bad you couldn't bear to look. Since I could move, I ran home.

My friends who'd been swimming naked mostly died in two or three days. Other classmates had been in the city helping demolish houses—most of them died too. If we hadn't been assigned air-defense duty, we'd have been with them and died for sure. My grade had four classes of 40 students each. Three-fourths of us died in the bombing.

Right after the explosion, you couldn't see a thing because of the smoke. Toward the hypocenter the smoke was surging, up and up. I can never forget the unearthly sight of the people who came up from Kusunoki-cho, washing their blood off in the river.

Just after the bombing, the school building was still standing. But everything around it burned until sparks got it and fire took it down. My house was damaged. At the time, we lived in staff housing for the driving school, where my dad worked. The lights wouldn't come on. For some nights, I don't know how many, we slept in the air-raid shelter.

didn't think seriously; they fooled themselves. "Okay, Hiroshima's gonna be fine." Then, that day . . .

It was the day after I turned 15.

We were out on the riverbank in front of the school waiting for class to start at 8:30—over ten of us, I guess. It was so hot, some boys jumped into the river—the Ota River.

The time was 8:15, but we only learned that later. I saw the plane that dropped it, you know. Came after the air-raid warning cleared.

Showed up so suddenly, didn't think it was an enemy plane. I only saw one. It came over Ushita into the city skies and headed to Iwakuni. . .

Just when I thought, "Hey, this is weird!" my head suddenly heated. The moment of explosion, for me, was the moment I thought, "Hot!" My student cap flew off, my hair caught fire. I had no idea what had happened. I could still hear the engine drone, so I was just getting ready to jump in the river, but then I saw my friends who were in the water—they were horribly burned. The skin had cleanly peeled off

Bombed the day after he turned 15 (Tetsuo Ikegami)

When I was born we lived on the streetcar street at Hondori 9-chome in Kure City. Because my father was a policeman, he was often transferred. We soon moved to Koi (now, koi, Nishi-ku, Hiroshima City) and I went to Koi Elementary until I was in the second or third grade. Then we moved to Oshiba (now, Oshiba, Nishi-ku, Hiroshima City). I went to Oshiba Elementary School and Sotoku Junior High School.

By the time, enemy planes were regularly attacking the homeland. I think the bosses knew, "We're not gonna win this." Students had to work outside as members of the air defense brigade—not much schoolwork going on. Every day, the ones living close by were mobilized for air-raid defense duty at school.

Until the atomic bombing, Hiroshima had hardly been hit, while American planes were always flying over Kure, because it was a key naval base. So people musician. His intellect was equivalent to that of a seven- or eight-year-old, but he loved classical music and had perfect pitch. Any melody he heard once he could play on the accordion without sheet music.

In 2009, Fu-chan died at age 63. For our two children, I feel that growing up with Fu-chan was "peace education" in the truest sense.

I think my father, who had said little about his A-bomb experience, overcame his resistance to talk to us because he wants the peace we enjoy today to continue.

Peace is number one. I feel keenly that we must expand the power of peace through steady dialogue.

Feeling anew the importance of conveying this tragic story to future generations, my wife and I collaborated to interview and bring you his words just as he spoke them.

Reflections upon completing the written version of my father's story
(Kozo Ikegami)

I was in elementary school the first time my father (Tetsuo Ikegami) told me about the atomic bombing. He responded to my request to interview him for an anti-war book our school was making. I remember that as I listened and wrote down the story of my father's A-bomb experience more than 40 years ago, I got very angry at the injustice.

Born on August 5th, 1930, he suffered the bombing the day after his 15th birthday. On August 5th, 2015, he was 85.

I have never suffered discrimination or bullying as a second-generation survivor. I have never suffered health effects. My life has been almost too normal.

My family took my Uncle Fumio (Fu-chan) to live with us in Fukuyama. Fu-chan was born with Down's syndrome caused by in-utero exposure. He lived with us for 24 years. Fu-chan was a fine

Families Look at August 6, 1945

Peace is number one. May steady dialogue expand the power of peace.

Kozo Ikegami

Sumiyo Ikegami

Tetsuzo Ikegami

(Fukuyama City, Hiroshima Prefecture)

to hear from them become fewer. When I showed this text to my mother, she cried, and August 6 appeared in her dream again that night. This is the "raw voice" of a survivor.

I hope everyone will listen to the heartrending cries of survivors and their children. In particular, I hope young people will do so as long as it is possible.

good answers, The atomic bomb and the war keep torturing not only survivors but also their descendants, even after 70 years.

Prejudice and discrimination against survivors, and second generation survivors, has diminished. We are slowly creating the conditions for all of us to think together about our problems. But do non-survivors know that survivors and second generation survivors are still having regular medical examinations?

Hijiyama Hill, where my mother rested after the bombing, is now a nice park. In one corner of that park stands a facility called the Radiation Effects Research Foundation (RERF). RERF examines and studies survivors looking for aftereffects. It takes about a month after each examination to get the results. While waiting for those results, I never feel really alive. I keep thinking, "What if they found some A-bomb disease?"

I want so badly for people to hear the "raw voices" of survivors. They are aging and every year the chances

My thought as a second generation survivor

I will turn now to myself. I was born twelve years after the bombing on April 4, 1957. I grew up in Hiroshima and have heard about the atomic bombing often. It seems to me that I became aware of myself as a "second generation survivor" when I entered junior high school, but I didn't willingly let anyone know.

I had a sad experience after graduating from high school and starting a new job. My friend reported that her acquaintance, someone I had never met, said, "Is she from Hiroshima? Then her parents must be survivors, right?" She was talking about me, and if I had heard her, I would have been deeply hurt.

I keep many things in my mind as a second generation survivor, but my feelings are quite complicated. For example, I sometimes wonder why was Hiroshima, home to my parents, had to be targeted. But, do I wish some other city had been targeted? (How could I?) This is one of several conundrums to which I have never found

My mother's hometown was Miyoshi City, but she had come to Hiroshima to earn money. She suffered bad burns on her head, the back of her neck, her elbow and below her knee. Still, she went home before long. She separated from the two friends who were with her at the time of the bombing and learned later that both of them died. When I asked how they died, she said she didn't know. Since all three were exposed at the same time and place, I'm sure she was afraid to know.

At 27, my mother married my father, who was also an A-bomb survivor. They worked hard to bring us up. When August 6 approached, she would also say, "I still have nightmares about that bombing." The atomic bombing is lodged in my mother's mind even now.

My mother's most moving words were, "We didn't experience that bomb because we wanted to, you know." I want people around the world to know the horror of the bomb that made her say those painful words so intensely.

When she came to she was covered in blood. She didn't feel pain in that instant, but, "As time went by, the pain got worse."

I asked, "What did you do then?" She said, "I didn't think about my body at all. I was simply stunned that the whole city had disappeared." She said the entire city on the other side of the bridge was gone without a trace.

People around the bridge began jumping in the river. Her friends saw them and urged her to go into the river as well, but my mother said, "No, I don't want to go into the river. Let's go back to Toyo Kogyo." So the three of them fled toward Hijiyama Hill.

Thousands of people took refuge on Hijiyama Hill. They met a Toyo Kogyo employee who took my mother and her friends to a dormitory. Many people exposed to the bombing were already on the grounds of the dormitory. Mother said, "Many of them were dead." The dead were piled into what seemed like mountains of corpses.

The day my mother was bombed

I will tell my mother's atomic bomb experience to the extent that I know it.

Her name was Masako Takasaka. On August 6 1945, she was 15 years old and working for Toyo Kogyo (now, Mazda). But for five days, starting that day, she and two friends were scheduled to help with building demolition.

My mother arrived at Mukainada Railway Station to catch a train leaving at 7:50. One of her friends came late so they missed that train. That was the moment that decided her fate.

My mother was exposed to the bombing while walking with her two friends along the bank of Kyobashi River from Hiroshima Station toward Tsurumi Bridge (now, Naka-ku, Hiroshima City), 18 kilometers from the hypocenter.

An air-raid warning cleared as they approached the bridge. She took off her air-raid hood and looked up the sky. Suddenly, an intense ray of light hit her from the back. A blast knocked her unconscious.

Families Look at August 6, 1945

Please listen to the heartrending cry of a survivor and her family.

 **Keiko Oe**

 **Masako Kousaka**

(Hatsukaichi City, Hiroshima Prefecture)

CONTENTS

Preface 4

Keiko Oe / Masako Kousaka 10

Kozo Ikegami / Sumiyo Ikegami / Tetsuzo Ikegami 18

Tatsuko Ota 26

Takashi Katsunori / Michiko Katsunori 36

Sachiko Nakanishi 50

Tokutomo Hase / Tsuchio Hase 58

Michiaki Fujii / Kazuko Fujii 66

Kazutoshi Nakamura 76

Masaichi Egawa 82

Teruo Tomita 94

In Closing 102

held Hiroshima Study Lecture Series for Peace—more than 160 since 1989. Clearly, young people are taking up the banner.

Seventy years after the bombing, with the average age of the hibakusha now over 80, every related organization is grappling with the critical question of how to pass on the experience.

Passion for nuclear abolition and the spirit of Hiroshima passed from parent to child, then inspired youths to create this book. We hope their book will help that passion grow into a universal value.

October 2015
70 years after atomic bombing

Kimio Yodoya
Chair of Hiroshima Youth Peace Committee
of Soka Gakkai

Sachie Hirai
Chair of Hiroshima Women's Peace and
Culture Conference of Soka Gakkai

world utterly devoid of the light of human feeling. A living hell. We have no way to communicate this, so we remain silent. All survivors bear these wounds of the heart."

His anguished cry smites our hearts. Nonetheless, rather than turning away from the past, we believe that people who face reality and allow the resulting pain into their hearts can take the first step toward creating a world free of war and nuclear weapons.

People created our foolish history of war.

Thus, people must create a history of peace.

Who are the people?

Must they not be the youth, who have the mission and responsibility of living in the future?

If even one youth burns with a passion for peace like the fire that motivated the ten children who launched the movement to preserve the A-bomb Dome, that youth can change the world. In the past and now, the key change agents are young people.

The experiences and thoughts printed here were heard and recorded by the youth. The Soka Gakkai Hiroshima Youth Peace Conference have regularly grateful that a movement begun by ten students spread like wildfire and culminated in preserving the structure in perpetuity.

Families Look at August 6 — Ten Accounts to Pass Forward compiles the A-bomb experiences collected by the Hiroshima Youth Peace Conference (members of the Youth Peace Committee, the Women's Peace and Culture Conference, and the Student Peace Committee). The accounts were collected by visiting the homes of hibakusha and asking them to take part in the project. Four of the accounts are presented in the voices of the hibakusha. The other six offer something quite new: they carry and blend the voices of a hibakusha and a second-generation hibakusha—namely, that person's child.

The sharing of these stories brings pain to both teller and listener. One of the hibakusha cries, "Hibakusha don't enjoy sharing their experiences because we don't want to cry. The catastrophe was just too cruel, too horrible for words. It was a dark cho, Aki-gun, Hiroshima Prefecture, had died of acute leukemia at age 16. The ten children were elementary, junior high, and high school student members of the Hiroshima Paper Crane Association. They were moved by Hiroko's diary. Beads of sweat dotted their foreheads as they passed out flyers that included a quote from Hiroko: "After the 20th century, will only the pledge on the Cenotaph for the A-bomb Victims and the piteous A-bomb Dome eternally continue to convey the horrifying atomic bombing to the world?"

The general public tended to oppose the preservation. Opinions were divided even among the hibakusha. The major newspapers advocated removal. The mayor of Hiroshima and prefectural governor called for tearing the ruins down. Despite the prevalent mood, the Hiroshima Paper Crane Association started the movement and gradually won support from various groups and notable persons. In July 1966, the Hiroshima City Council unanimously adopted a resolution committing the city to preserving the A-bomb Dome. I am deeply

Preface

One hundred years ago, in 1915, the structure we call the A-bomb Dome opened its doors as the Hiroshima Prefectural Commercial Exhibition Hall. Its purpose was to promote local products. In later years, it was renamed the Hiroshima Prefectural Industrial Promotion Hall.

At 8:15 on August 6, 1945, the world's first atomic bomb exploded 600 meters over a point 160 meters southeast of that building. Now, the A-bomb Dome is a designated World Heritage, but at one point, it seemed bound to collapse.

August 1960. Six years before Hiroshima City launched its first A-bomb Dome preservation funding drive, ten children standing in front of the Children's Peace Monument in Peace Memorial Park asked passersby to donate money and sign a petition calling for preservation of the ruins.

In April that year, Hiroko Kajiyama of Fuchu-

Families Look at August 6, 1945

Ten Accounts to Pass Forward

DAISANBUNMEI-SHA
TOKYO

Copyright © 2015 Soka Gakkai Hiroshima Youth Division

Published in 2015
by Daisanbunmei-sha,Inc.
1-23-5 Shinjuku Shinjuku-ku,Tokyo Japan
http://www.daisanbunmei.co.jp

家族から見た「8・6」
──語り継ぎたい10の証言

2015年11月18日　初版第1刷発行

編　者	創価学会広島青年部
発行者	大島光明
発行所	株式会社　第三文明社 東京都新宿区新宿1-23-5 郵便番号：160-0022 電話番号：03（5269）7145（営業代表） 　　　　　03（5269）7154（編集代表） 振替口座　00150-3-117823 URL http://www.daisanbunmei.co.jp
英語翻訳	澤田美和子／エリザベス・ボールドウィン
装幀・本文DTP	木村祐一（株式会社ゼロメガ）
印刷・製本	藤原印刷株式会社

©Soka Gakkai 2015　　　　　　　　　　　　　　Printed in Japan
ISBN978-4-476-06228-1

乱丁・落丁本はお取り換えいたします。ご面倒ですが、小社営業部宛お送りください。
送料は当方で負担いたします。
法律で認められた場合を除き、本書の無断複写・複製・転載を禁じます。